COASTAL SKIPPER
SAILING

Coastal Skipper
Sailing

Karle Stephenson

The Crowood Press

First published in 1998 by
The Crowood Press Ltd
Ramsbury, Marlborough
Wiltshire SN8 2HR

British Library Cataloguing in Publication Data

A catalogue record for this book is available from the British Library.

ISBN 1 86126 035 0

Line drawings by Andrew Green and David Fisher.

Acknowledgements
Many thanks to my friend and colleague Bob Mills, who kindly read the text and made valuable comments upon it.

Typeset by Annette Findlay
Printed and bound in Great Britain by WBC Book Manufacturers Ltd., Mid Glamorgan

CONTENTS

Yacht – sailing

1
SAILS AND SAILING

The History of Sailing

The square sail is the oldest type of sail that we know; it is still used today, and is often seen on large sail training yachts. It is attached to a horizontal pole or yard and suspended from a single mast. The fundamental feature of a square sail is that the same side is always faced to the wind, and the yacht to which it is attached is simply pushed downwind.

A model of a yacht with such a sail, representing an elaborately decorated vessel of some one hundred feet in length, was found in the tomb of an Egyptian nobleman of the eighteenth dynasty; the original vessel was probably sailed down the Nile on the prevailing wind, only to be rowed back by a crew of slaves at some later date. This model certainly indicates that sailing with a single square sail was well advanced some 1,500 years B.C., and in fact Egyptian clay urns dated to some 4,000 years B.C. have been found with painted representations of boats carrying a single square sail. At a later date Cleopatra's square-sailed barge was said by Plutarch to have been very beautiful, with a poop of gold, purple sails and silver oars, from which we may infer that sailing was well established by this time.

Centuries of development in masts and rigging led to the design of yards, which could be angled across the boat. The yard was hauled around using a bowline, literally a line attached to the bow of the vessel; in this way the single square sail hung from the yard gave some 'weatherliness' to the boat – weatherliness being that ability to sail on a broad reach rather than merely being able to run downwind. The original appearance of the bowsprit may well have been to give a more effective forward lead to the bowlines.

Early Greek manuscripts show sailing craft fitted with a triangular sail under an inclined yard: known as the lateen sail, the origins of the design are unknown, although it is the first evidence of a fore-and-aft sail. Its big disadvantage is that since it is carried forward of the mast, the whole sail must be carried around the front of the mast when tacking.

In the sixteenth century the Dutch needed to sail much closer to the wind than hitherto, and to this end designed two new fore-and-aft sails: the spritsail and the staysail.

1) The spritsail, set abaft the mast, is a simple square-shaped sail with the leading edge laced to the mast; it is held aloft

by a diagonally placed spar called the sprit, the heel of which is pivoted at the bottom of the mast and attached to the sail's bottom corner, extending it into its square shape.

2) The triangular staysail, often called the fore-staysail, was shaped to fit on the forward side of the mast under the fore-stay. This sail was quickly followed by a second staysail called the 'jib', set onto a 'jib-boom' outside the stem. Other designs of fore-and-aft rig include the fixed and the dipping lug, and the gunter and the gaff main. Fig.1 shows a silhouette of these various sail shapes.

Before ending this brief history on sail development it is perhaps worth mentioning that the requirements of trade and expansion led to ships having several masts and many sails. The paradigm of sailing ship design was probably the three-masted, square-rigged ship that was to conquer the seas and oceans of the world. Such vessels carried several square sails on the fore and main masts, a lateen on the mizzen with a square above it, and fore-staysails on the bowsprit. The English battleship *Sovereign of the Sea* of 1637 (Fig. 2) was the biggest ship in the world at that time, and she carried four square sails on her fore and main masts, a lateen and upper square on her mizzen, with bow-spritsail and several fore-stay-sails on her bowsprit. You can imagine the enormous number of ropes necessary to support and manage such massive configurations of timber and canvas, all of which had individual names and uses; spare a thought for the poor midshipman, who by means of candlelight and the gen-

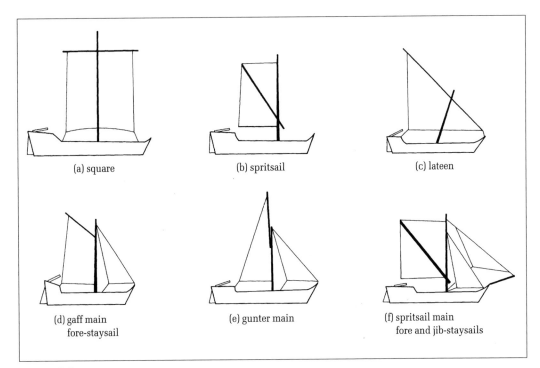

(a) square

(b) spritsail

(c) lateen

(d) gaff main
fore-staysail

(e) gunter main

(f) spritsail main
fore and jib-staysails

Fig.1 Sail shapes.

Fig. 2 *Sovereign of the Sea.*

tle persuasion of the bosun's rope end, needed to commit all these names to memory.

Modern Yacht Rigs

The staysail – a triangular sail set on a stay, or one having a luff rope with its own halyard – appeared quite suddenly, and there are no records of it having developed from earlier designs. It is indisputably a very efficient sail, and made its relatively late appearance in the fifteenth or sixteenth century in the English channel. Designed by the Dutch, it was of the fore-and-aft family, fitting neatly into that space before the mast. Originally set to assist in manoeuvring the boat's head round when tacking, the staysail was aerodynamically superior to any previous design, although this was not appreciated at the time, and significantly improved manoeuvrability; moreover as we shall see, the act of lacing this sail to the forestay was one of unintentional genius.

Sailing for pleasure in UK waters began in the early seventeenth century when King Charles and his brother were each presented with new yachts. Designed in England, these were based on an earlier Dutch East India Company yacht called *The Mary*, presented to the king in 1660.

Sailing, cruising and racing became ever more popular, and improvements in hull construction and sail design continued apace; and then in the early 1690s, in Bermuda, an American yacht architect called William Gardener set a triangular mainsail onto a one-piece mast. This rig became known as the Bermudian sloop, and it is upon this basic concept that most modern yachts are designed. From Fig. 1 above, it may now seem to be a very small step from the gunter-rigged main, with its heavy top spar and necessary hoisting tackles; but someone had to take that step, and yachting history attributes this achievement to William. It may well have been that the sailing fraternity of those days was just beginning to recognize the aerofoil behaviour of shaped fore-and-aft sails, and that this led to his single mast design. Whatever the reason, a Bermudian rigged sloop was not only much faster to windward than any previous sail plan but, more importantly, she could sail much closer to the wind.

Sail Trim

Both jib and mainsail are basically triangular, but most significantly each has a characteristic curve to its shape, built in by the skill of the sailmaker; it is this shaping which allows the yachtie to present the sail as an aerofoil section to the wind. Each side and each corner of the sail has its own identifying name, as indicated in Fig. 3.

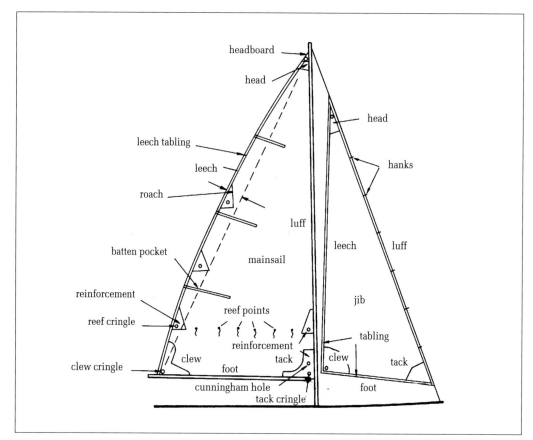

Fig.3 Jib and mainsail.

Foresail or Jib

The jib has a sewn-in cringle at each corner allowing for the attachment of the halyard, at the head; the foretack shackle at the tack; and the two sheets, 'working' and 'lazy', at the clew. The luff is fitted with spring-loaded 'piston shanks', sewn into the sailcloth for attaching the luff of the sail to the forestay.

To hoist the foresail it is removed from its own bag, 'bent on' at the tack and luff, and the two sheets are then 'bowlined' onto the clew and led aft. The halliard, with its shackle attached to the head of the sail, is then used to haul the sail aloft. In leading the two attached sheets aft, one down each side-deck of the yacht, they are first passed through a movable spring-loaded 'car', thence through a deck-mounted turning block, and so onto their own coach-roof winch; finally a stopper knot is tied at the bitter end of each sheet to prevent it running back through the turning blocks. (See Fig. 4.)

Under jib only, the main neatly furled.

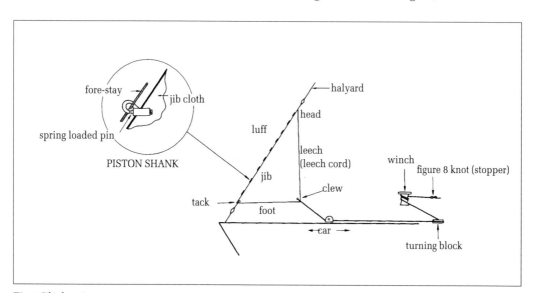

Fig. 4 Jib sheeting.

Most yachts carry several jibs: a small storm-sail of heavy material; a working jib (this is the work-horse of jibs, being of a size to 'balance' the mainsail in normal to strong wind strengths); and a set of three genoas of increasing size, number one genoa being the largest sail. Genoas have a much longer foot length than the working jib, giving them a degree of overlap to the mainsail; they are used with a full main in light to moderate wind strengths.

The Mainsail

Fig. 3 illustrates the triangular shape of the main with its named sides and corners, also its built-in aerofoil shape. Unlike foresails, which are constantly being changed to meet the varying wind strengths and are generally stowed at the end of the day, the main is semi-permanently fixed to the boom. In most cases this is by means of a sail 'foot-rope', which slides in a groove along the top of the boom; the tack cringle is effectively attached to the mast, enabling the foot of the main to be hauled taut by means of the 'outhaul': this is a rope led from the clew cringle, through a turning-block sheave fitted into the end of the boom, and brought back inside the boom to the mast where it can be winched and cleated.

In most modern yachts the main is attached to the mast by means of 'sliders' sewn at intervals into the luff of the main and slotted into a 'T'-shaped slot in the stern face of the mast; this allows the main to be hauled aloft by its own halliard. Fig. 5 shows three reefing cringles sewn into the leech and the luff of the sail – you will notice that the two lower leech reefing cringles are fitted with their own 'reefing pennants'. These are ropes which are first bent onto the boom immediately below their respective cringles, led up through that cringle, then passed back to the mast, in exactly the same way as the outhaul discussed earlier. It follows that as the wind strength increases, the effective size of the main can be reduced in three stages. Fig. 5 also shows the 'topping lift', a rope which is attached to the end of the boom, led up to a block at the top of the mast, then down the inside of the mast to emerge at about waist height to its own cleat. The topping lift is used whenever the boom is not being supported by a wind-filled mainsail, for example when reefing.

If the weather worsens when sailing under full main, the skipper may decide to put in one reef, and to do this he will proceed as follows: first, the head of the yacht is brought into wind or the yacht is 'hove to'. Next, the weight of the boom is taken up on the 'topping lift', then the halliard is eased allowing the main to be pulled down until the first, lower, luff cringle can be 'caught' on the 'ram's horn' fitting. The halliard is hauled taught again, and the first reefing pennant is hauled taught in order to tighten the foot of the sail, and is cleated off. The reefing points along the reduced sail are 'reef-knotted' to the boom, and finally the topping lift is eased off as the yacht sails away under reduced main.

Should the skipper delay reefing until late in an increasing wind strength, the crew may be less fortunate in that the reefing operation must now be from full main to the third reef in one invariably nerve-racking operation. In this case the first necessary action is to re-run the lower reefing pennant to the third cringle, and then reef. In fact you would have

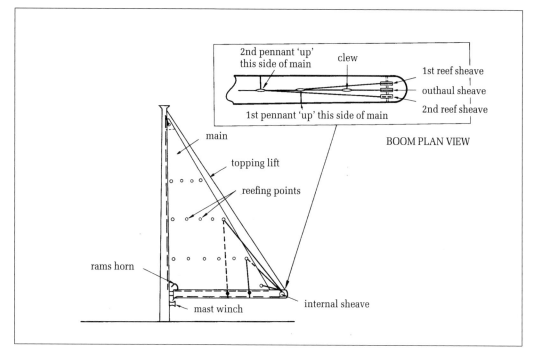

Fig. 5 Reefing cringles and pennants.

every good reason to ask first, why the skipper left it so late before reefing, and second, why he didn't fit three reefing pennants?

There is really *no* good reason, when cruising, to delay reefing, and the time to reef is the moment the thought first crosses your mind; after all, you can always shake out a reef if the really bad weather does not materialize. The reason for not running three reefing pennants is that most yachts are only fitted with a three-sheave block in the end of the boom – Fig. 5 – and one is required for the out-haul. The lower two pennants are usually the ones rigged because normally in con-ditions when the wind is increasing, the skipper who loves his crew would be careful to avoid the following sequence of events:

The wind builds up, and the yacht, with its genoa and full main beautifully balanced until now, with only a finger-tip required on the tiller to keep her on course, develops weather helm. That is, she tries to head into the wind, with the poor helm having to grip the tiller harder and harder and at a greater angle in order to keep her on course. If nothing is done to relieve the situation the lee rail will be under water and any gust will broach the boat.

The caring skipper, however, will be well aware of the wind increase and the developing sail imbalance, and will reduce the strength of the main by reef-ing. This may result in the genoa being the dominant sail, in which case it will be exchanged for a smaller genoa or the working jib. Whether reefing the main or reducing the size of the jib, the aim is to maintain a balanced rig.

In general, the sequence of events would probably follow this sort of order:

Developing weather helm? If yes, the main will be taken from full to first reef. Then sail a while, watching the weather. Does the jib need to be reduced? If yes, do so.

Is weather helm still a problem? If yes, first reef to second, and now re-run the first pennant to become the third. Sail a while again watching the weather: does the jib need to be reduced further? If yes, do so.

Weather helm still a problem? If yes, second reef to third reef.

It is still necessary to re-run the pennant, but you don't have to fight a full-sized main down to minimum in one go.

A second reason for rigging the first and second pennants is that the weight of these two pennant ropes is put at the lowest possible place on the leech – although in light winds, even with the weight of these ropes at the minimum height, the leech may not set properly; however, you should *never* be tempted to remove them altogether, even in the lightest of winds.

Whenever a mainsail has to be fitted, or refitted to the boom, make sure that the outhaul runs over the centre sheave of the three, and that the first and second pennants are 'run up' opposite sides of the mainsail, then each taken to 'that side's' sheave, otherwise they will jam in use.

There is still a great deal of discussion about 'how sails sail', and what follows is the author's understanding of this controversial topic, an understanding developed over many years of reading, argument and experience, and particularly argument. Fig. 6 shows the air streams about a shaped sail in which the luff edge has been hauled taut. At point (a) the air flow has no knowledge of the presence of the sail; however, it is definitely disturbed as it splits on approaching the sail, some flowing over its lee side and the rest over its windward side. At point (b) the air flow has returned to the same flow behaviour and pressures as at point (a). The following facts of air flow should be appreciated before reading further:

1) When an air stream is constricted in flowing over an aerofoil-shaped sail, its speed increases.

2) When air-stream speed increases in flowing over an aerofoil-shaped sail, the pressure falls.

3) When air-stream speed over an aerofoil-shaped sail falls too quickly, air pressure rises too quickly, and the air stream will separate from the sail which will 'stall' and lose power. Separation does not occur when pressure is falling.

Consider now the air flow on the lee side of the sail: as the air approaches the luff it cannot/doesn't make a sudden sharp turn, it bends to its new lee-side direction, and this bending must start somewhere in front of the luff edge, as shown. The lee air flow increases in speed as it bends around the luff, and it continues to increase in speed until it reaches the deepest part of the draft or camber of the sail; from this point its speed falls until, at the leech of the sail, it is back to the same uninterrupted flow rate as at (a).

Consider now the windward air flow: this slows as it enters the area behind the sail and moves across it, and it continues to lose speed, and therefore to increase in pressure, up to the point of deepest camber; after this point it increases speed until at the leech it rejoins the lee-side air

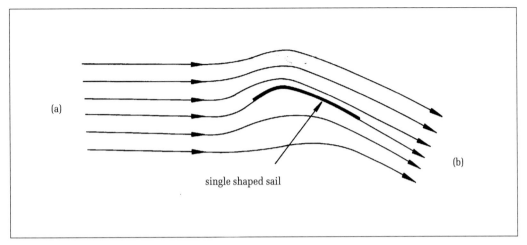

Fig. 6 Air streams about a single sail.

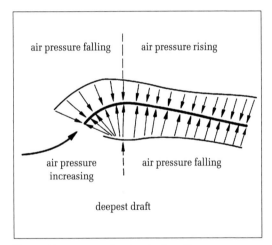

Fig. 7 Air pressure about a single sail.

at 'free air speed'. Fig. 7 shows that as the air speed increases over the lee side of the sail up to the point of maximum camber, the air pressure acting on this area of the sail falls, then increases towards the leech as the corresponding air flow falls back to 'normal' air speed. On the windward side the pressure acting on the sail increases up to the maximum camber and then falls back to normal as it flows to the leech.

It is the air pressure difference between the lee and windward sides of the sail that produces lift, as shown at Fig. 8. Maximum lift occurs from the luff to the deepest point of camber, although some lift occurs right across the lee side of the

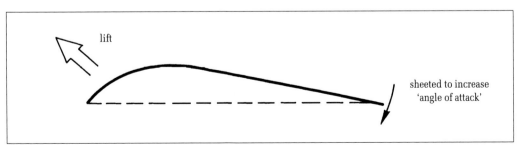

Fig. 8 Sail lift.

sail. If the camber of the sail is increased or developed too far back in the sail, thus reducing the distance in which the air speed must reduce to the free air speed, the increase in pressure would cause separation and the sail would 'stall'. The art of sail trim is to so arrange the amount and direction of this lift that the boat moves forwards at the maximum speed.

Luffing and Stalling

The basic camber of the sail is built into it by the sailmaker, but the sailor has some control over the position of the maximum camber, in that increasing the halliard tension will move it forwards and flatten the sail; it also frees the leech.

In the case of the jib, moving the car block forwards from its normal position, where it causes the jib sheet to bisect the included sail angle of the clew, will increase the tension of the leech and thereby move the point of maximum camber aft and ease both the luff and the foot of the sail; easing of the luff and the foot puts more of a 'bag' into the sail's shape. Moving the car aft eases the leech, the camber moves forwards in the sail, and the foot tension is increased.

When sailing to windward, or beating, the helm points the yacht as close to the direction from which the wind is coming as the sails will allow; in a well suited and set up boat he will be able to tack through 90 degrees – that is, 45 degrees to the true wind on each tack. Attempting to sail closer than this will cause the sail to luff: that is, the air stream will be caused to flow more directly at the lee side of the sail, literally striking the lee of the sail at the luff, and this will cause it first to lift and then to shake as the boat is brought

further into the wind. For a yacht to beat as close as possible in a strong wind, the halliard is set taut, the car moved aft and the sheet brought in tight; this will put the point of maximum camber approximately one third of the sail's width in from the luff. Should the helm lose concentration when beating and allow the head to move 'off the wind', the lee-side air stream will separate from the sail as it moves from the point of maximum camber towards the leech, and the sail is then said to have 'stalled'. The windward air stream will increasingly strike more directly against the sailcloth, thus increasing the heeling movement and reducing the forward thrust. Luffing or stalling the yacht will lose forward drive and slow the speed considerably.

When beating in light winds the halliard should be set less taut, and the foot eased by moving the car block forwards, thus allowing the camber to move aft and the sail to 'bag' slightly. Light air streams over the lee of the sail are thereby given more sail length to accelerate over, producing a lower pressure over a greater area; these lighter winds are not so likely to separate on the lee side as they flow to the leech. Light air streams on the windward side are also given more length, in this case in which to decelerate, producing a greater area of increased pressure.

Fig. 9 shows a yacht beating to windward with the jib hauled in taut; very little camber is shown, the aim of course being to get the boat as close to the wind as possible (45 degrees to the true wind). In Fig. 9 the direction of the air-pressure thrust acting on the sail is f2, the two resultant vectors f1 and f3 representing the forward and heeling thrust respectively. Forward thrust is what we want, heeling thrust is what we have to put up

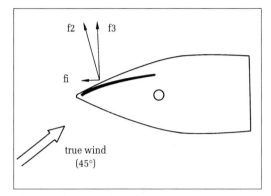

Fig. 9 Beating to windward.

with. Notice that most of the air-pressure thrust is developed as a heeling moment, and that very little is converted into forward thrust.

Sail Interaction

When both main and overlapping jib are set they act together as one aerofoil section, and the air stream approaching the main/jib combination splits into three flows, each with a different influence according to where they make contact with the sails; thus:

1) The windward side of the main receives air very much like a single sail.
2) The area between the sails is more complex in that the space for the air stream to flow into is reduced, and reduces further as the leech of the jib is approached. This constriction between forestay and mast also forces more air over the lee side of the sail combination than would flow over the lee side of a single jib. Consequently the smaller volume of air passing into this 'slot' is flowing more slowly over the leeward side of the main and the windward side of the jib

than for single sails, pressure on these areas of the sails is thus higher, and the luff of the jib gets more lift and the main less. As the slot tightens towards the leech of the jib the air accelerates, moving faster than the free air speed experienced by the leech of a jib alone. Air in this relatively high-pressure area between the sails accelerating towards the slot gives reduced pressure on both the lee side of the main and the windward side of the jib; this means that the lift on the lee side of the main is improving, and it also means that separation on this sail will not occur. However, the pressure difference across the jib is reducing.

3) Air flow over the lee side of the jib is greater, air speed is therefore higher and pressure lower than would be the case of the jib alone, giving more lift. Finally the increased speed of air through the slot allows the jib's lee air to decelerate at a lower rate than normal, thus reducing the risk of separation.

In summary, the main sail/genoa combination, in causing a greater diversion and volume of the air stream to flow to the lee of the jib, allows the yacht to point closer to wind, and the increased air velocities over the leech of the jib and the body of the main allow for greater angles of attack before stalling occurs.

In beating to windward the helmsman's limits are that if he sails too close to the wind the sails will luff, and if he bears away they will stall.

We make to windward because the wind is coming from where we want to go. A well trimmed jib/main combination will make a 90-degree tack a possibility, and because this combination is less likely to stall than a single sail, you will be able to 'fall off the wind' a little –

accidently of course – without the crew even noticing.

Tell-Tales

Tell-tales are ribbons of lightweight cloth sewn into the luff of the jib and the leech of the main; they are usually made from spinnaker sailcloth, and normally three are fitted to each sail. On the jib they are positioned just above the foot, halfway up the sail and just below the head, and they are fitted to both sides of the jib cloth about 6in (15cm) in from the luff rope. The lee-side tell-tales will twirl when the sail is sheeted in too hard or when the yacht is too far off the wind, and the windward tell-tales twirl when the sheet is eased too much or the boat is too close to the wind; but note that if they indicate like this you have probably already sailed too close to windward or fallen too far off the wind. We have already noted that when too close to windward the sail will luff, too far off and it will stall – either way it is losing pulling power. We also noted that the approaching wind splits, some to be bent round to the lee of the sail, the rest to flow into the windward side. When the sails are correctly trimmed and the boat is on the correct point of sail, the air flow will be smooth on both sides of the sail; this is called a laminar flow, and all the tell-tales will fly cleanly off the jib sailcloth and stream out straight behind the main.

Thus the windward jib tell-tales twirl at the onset of luffing, and their dance may well be accompanied by the head of the jib lifting. However, it is much more important to take action when the lee-side tell-tales start twirling because this happens when the jib is about to stall – it

is an early warning that separation turbulence has started at the fore lee of the jib.

Apparent Wind

From the hypotheses above, we have seen that a well set up sailing yacht can make to windward at an angle of 45 degrees to the wind. However, to the sailor on board the wind will appear to be coming from almost dead ahead, and in fact all indicators – ensigns, burgees, even the wind on your face – tell you that the wind is coming from much further ahead than 45 degrees. This 'onboard wind' is called 'apparent wind' and is due to the yacht's forward movement, and it is important to understand how it is generated: in fact it is a combination of the true wind – that is, the wind experienced when the yacht is stationary, ie at anchor – and the wind 'made' by the sailing yacht in simply moving forwards.

Any boat, power or sail, when it is moving ahead will feel a headwind, even in still air – in fact any moving object creates its own wind. The speed of this 'made' wind is exactly equal to the speed of the boat through the air, so for instance a yacht beating 45 degrees to a true wind of 15 knots and making 5 knots through the wind, will generate its own 5 knot headwind. Fig. 10 illustrates this, and shows that the crew of such a yacht would experience an 'apparent wind' of 17 knots from a direction of 30 degrees. Apparent wind is always further 'ahead' than the true wind.

As another example, let us assume that a yacht is close-hauled on the starboard tack, with the wind apparently blowing from almost dead ahead. The skipper wishes to retrace his passage on the

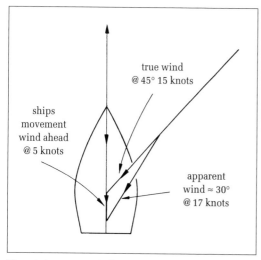

Fig. 10 Apparent wind.

reverse course, so what would be the 'point of sail' on the reverse passage? The answer is that the true wind would be abaft the port beam, with the apparent wind on the beam.

Points of Sail

A yacht is able to sail on all points of the compass except the 90 degrees of arc centred on the direction of the true wind. Fig. 11 illustrates and names some of these points.

On all points of sail, except when running which is explained below, the jib and main must be set up to attack the wind at exactly the same angle and shape as previously discussed; after all, the sail has no knowledge of the relative position of the boat's hull, it reacts only to the direction from which the wind is coming onto it. It is the helm's job simply to pivot the boat into the desired direction, and the crew's to adjust the ropes controlling the sails – the halliards, sheets, cars, outhauls and

leech lines – so as to set the sails into the wind. Notice in Fig. 11 that as the boat bears away from the wind the jib and main sheets must be eased to prevent the sails from stalling (to recap: stalling occurs when the luff angle forces too sharp a 'bend' to the wind moving over the lee side of the sail, so the wind simply detaches from the sail as it moves beyond the deepest point of the camber). The 'ideal' sail setting is just before the luff of the sail's lift, ie at the point of luffing.

On a broad reach, particularly as the boat direction approaches a run, some stalling is inevitable; and on a full downwind run both jib and main are completely stalled, the sails and therefore the yacht itself being simply pushed along by the wind.

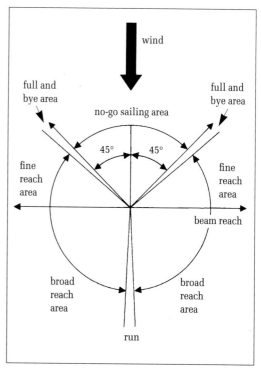

Fig. 11 Points of sail.

Running

When running downwind the boom is eased out until it almost touches the shrouds. By doing this the mainsail will be brought against the shrouds, and the resultant friction will inevitably cause wear; however, it is usually taken up by a protecting 'sacrificial wear' patch.

The jib sheet is eased out until the jib is lying across the wind, with the clew and tack in line at about 90 degrees to the wind; however, in this position the jib is completely screened from the wind and quite useless – it will simply flap around occasionally filling and then collapsing. The solution is to 'goosewing the jib' – that is, to haul in the lazy sheet so that the jib is pulled out to the opposite side of the yacht to which the main is set. The jib will now fill and fly under the control of its sheet alone; however, it is difficult to keep it filled in this way, and much easier to achieve if it is 'poled out'. On most cruising yachts the spinnaker pole is used for this purpose: it is first rigged on the opposite side to the boom, and is controlled vertically by the spinnaker up-and-down hauls, and horizontally by fore-and-aft guys run out specially. It should be positioned at right-angles to the boat, or hauled back as far as the shrouds permit. With the pole in position the jib can be hauled across using a new (second) lazy sheet.

It may seem here that a lot of trouble and rope is used to set up the pole, and certainly it takes time to do; however, it does mean that the pole is under complete control, and when coming off the run – that is, when moving onto a broad or beam reach – the now lazy sheet can be hauled in as normal to get the jib back on the 'right' side of the boat. The end of the boom can then be easily lowered, pulled forwards and secured at the bow for temporary stowage.

Avoid the practice of simply engaging the ends of the spinnaker pole into the working sheet of the goosewinged jib and its own mast fitting: no up- and down-hauls, no fore-and-aft pole guys, just the pole between mast and clew. It is a much quicker procedure, but *don't do it*: if the weather changes, disengaging that pole on a heaving deck could become a very dangerous job.

Two further points of safety need to be addressed:

(1) When running in an increasing wind, the yacht's speed can build up quite quickly, almost without the crew noticing; they may find that suddenly a big sea has developed, and that the boat is surfing along at high speed. Obviously the risk of her burying her bow as she runs down a large wave, with the consequent possibility of a broach and knockdown, increases with increasing wind strength and wave height.

(2) When running, the helm must be reasonably experienced because 'sailing by the lee' – when the wind gets behind the main – must not be allowed to occur; one possible consequence of this is an unexpected, uncontrolled and dangerous jibe in which the boom comes across the cockpit at a frightening speed taking anything in its path, before tearing away the shrouds on the opposite side, and the loose main sheet comes across the coach roof sweeping all before it over the side. Sailing by the lee on a full downwind run is therefore to be avoided, especially in a following sea when the boat may be yawing quite badly. However, the above

problems can be considerably reduced by sailing 10 degrees off a full 180-degree wind, and jibing round as necessary so that the average course is the one desired.

A jibe is a combined effort of helm and sheet-hand. The helm turns the stern through the wind 'gently' while the sheet-hand hauls in the sheet 'smartly', and their joint effort should ensure that as the stern is moved through the wind the boom is amidships; in a well controlled jibe it is possible at this time to sail downwind on the jib alone. To continue the jibe, the stern is moved through the wind and the sheet is eased until a 10-degree off-wind run is achieved on the other tack.

When cruising, a full 180-degree run is not necessary: the risks are too high. However, if it must be done, then consider using a 'preventer'. This is a rope which is led from an end or middle fitting under the boom, through a turning block secured forward, and thence to the cockpit where it is securely cleated in such a manner that it can be quickly released. Its name is certainly apt, because it does just that: prevents an unplanned jibe, since the boom simply cannot fly across the cockpit. Even so, it has its drawbacks: it can easily be forgotten and be still cleated when the skipper attempts a controlled jibe; or the wind may get behind the main, either because the boat is yawing in a following sea, or because of a sudden gust or wind change, and the boat may be knocked flat – and with the preventer doing its job, the sail will fill with water, the boat unable to recover...

So... 10 degrees off a full run is a good safety margin.

The Cruising Chute

A cruising chute is a foresail for the cruising sailor, lighter than the big genoas and much less demanding than the spinnaker. It is flown without a pole, and does not therefore require all the string that a safely poled out, goosewinged genoa needs. The chute is loose-luffed – that is, the luff is not attached to the forestay – because it is designed to fly ahead of the forestay and for that reason must be hoisted on the spinnaker halyard. A tack downhaul is attached using a snap shackle, then fed through a block at the bow before being led aft and secured. The sheet(s) are led to a turning block at the stern, outside everything, before being led to a convenient winch and cleat; the lazy sheet is passed in front of the forestay before being led aft.

When on a fine reach, if the yacht is to be tacked – when the head is put through the wind – the current working sheet must be let go and the lazy sheet used to haul the sail round the front of the forestay as the head moves through the wind. It should be noted here that in a normal tack the boat will be close-hauled and the jib, especially a big genoa, is tacked as the wind backs the sail; in this way the chances of a forestay wrap are minimized, and the sail moves across the boat quite quickly. However, when a chute is put across as the head goes through the wind, it has to be let go and literally hauled over by the sheet; and there is generally a great deal of sail material flapping around the forestay for some considerable time because the yacht would have been several degrees off the wind (ie not close-hauled). To prevent this happening, hoist a jib before attempting the tack: with this jib in the way a forestay wrap is impossible.

Jibing the chute is much easier: simply let go the working sheet and allow the chute to fly out ahead of the boat; put the stern through the wind, haul in the new working jib, and off you go on the new heading. Please note that for this operation the sheets need to be much longer than normal, at least equal in length to the boat plus the foot length of the chute plus a bit.

The cruising chute may be used from a full downwind run to a point were the wind is well ahead of the beam. It is not a good windward sail, although it is triangular and does have a luff edge. The finer the reach, the tighter the luff needs to be, and when the yacht bears away the halyard, tack downhaul and sheet are all eased until on a full run, with a mainsail preventer, the sail flying ahead with a deep, full-winded belly.

The chute should be hoisted behind a tightly sheeted jib to prevent it wrapping

Spinnaker run.

itself around the forestay; when it is sheeted in, the jib is dropped and packed away. To get the sail down, bring the boat onto a broad reach, then release the snap shackle at the tack, and haul in the sheet and then the clew, pulling the sail into the cabin for packing.

The Spinnaker

The spinnaker when set and properly flying provides one of the greatest pleasures of sailing; however, the exhilaration of seeing this wondrous billow of sail fill with wind is matched by the heart-squeezing knowledge that if you do not pay it the attention it requires then it will sulk, wrap itself around the forestay, and refuse to come unwrapped. It is a sail to be rigged and hoisted only by the experienced – and you get the experience from associating with the experienced. Spinnakers can be enormous, and when filling or filled with wind are very powerful. When flying on a full run the spinnaker tends to bury the yacht's bow, and you will see yachts with their entire crew in the aft part of the boat.

The sail is stowed in a specially designed bag called a 'turtle' which has a wired circular open rim, and when properly packed the head, clew and tack (the tack on a spinnaker is really a second clew) are immediately available for attachment when the turtle is undone. When aloft, the spinnaker flies ahead of the boat, so all ropes attached to it must be laid out prior to hoisting, to ensure that they are outside everything. The special spinnaker halyard masthead block is fitted at a higher position than the forestay. Each clew is fitted with its own sheet and guy rope, and in operation the working sheet and lazy guy on one clew are complemented by a working guy and lazy sheet on the opposite clew.

The spinnaker is rigged as follows: the yacht would be sailing normally with both main and jib. The spinnaker pole is first attached to its purpose-built fitting on the mast, the vertical position of which is adjustable, allowing it to be set so that the other end of the pole can rest on the deck at the bow, inside the pulpit, on the windward side. The spinnaker up- and downhauls are attached to their special pole fittings; note that the current lazy jib sheet must pass over the pole.

The turtle is attached to the forward guard rails under the jib, and is opened to expose only the head and clews of the sail. Halyard, sheets and guys are attached to the sail, and whoever has this task must be sure that he identifies the parts of the sail to be attached correctly otherwise he will have the embarrassment of finding that he is flying the spinnaker sideways.

The sheets and guys are led through their respective turning blocks, those for the guys somewhere astern of the mast, and those for the sheets as far aft as possible; they are then led to winches with convenient cleats. Before hoisting the sail, the windward sheet – attached as it is to the clew of the sail as it peeps out from the turtle – must be 'caught' in the spring-loaded fitting at the end of the pole.

All is now ready for the hoist. Put the yacht onto a full or nearly full run. Ideally there should be enough crew so that the working guy, working sheet, halyard, up- and downhauls, spinnaker pole and helm are all attended. I have to write this as a sequence, but several things will be done at the same time:

1) Hoist the spinnaker.
2) Haul the spinnaker pole to a horizontal position.
3) Haul in the guy and take in the slack on the working sheet; hauling in the guy will bring the spinnaker pole aft, continue hauling until the pole is roughly in line with the mainsail boom. Adjust the spinnaker pole's mast-fitting height so that it roughly equals the height of the guyed clew.
4) Tension the sheet to allow the spinnaker to fill.
5) Drop the jib.

1 and 2 above should be completed before any real tension is taken on the guy and sheet; these and 3 above are all done at the same time.

Setting the spinnaker pole in line with the main boom is the default position, and when the boat is only lightly crewed this is good enough. However the sheet, like all sheets, needs to be played with continuously – essentially it should be eased until the head of the sail at the trailing edge just folds, when it should be hauled in a little.

Getting the spinnaker down is done by allowing the boom to go forwards so that the guy shackle can be let go. With the shackle released at the 'tack' the sail will fly ahead and is pulled into the cabin, under the boom, by hauling in the sheet whilst lowering the halyard.

The procedure for packing cruising chutes and spinnakers is similar. Once pulled down into the cabin the head is found and temporarily tied to a deckhead fitting. Each edge of the sail is followed down to the respective clew, with the body of the sail lying in between; the clews are then tied to the suspended head so that all three corners are together with the rest of the sail – perhaps in an untidy mess, but one in which there cannot be any twists lying on the cabin floor. Pack the body of the sail into the turtle with the three corners, still held together, going in last.

Heaving To

When a yacht heaves to it ends up moving at less than one knot at some 60 degrees to the wind, a situation which facilitates a number of activities. For instance, it allows the mainsail to be reduced more easily when bad weather is building; the jib is still under wind pressure however, and so is not flapping around the ears of the crew working at the mast. Heaving to also allows the crew a brief respite on a long beat to windward, so they can enjoy a meal break with the boat sitting upright. Let us assume that a yacht close-hauled on the port tack is about to heave to; the skipper might explain the procedure as follows:

The helm will bring the yacht's head through the wind by moving the tiller to starboard – that is, to the lee side of the boat – as if tacking; however, the working jib sheet will not be released. As the head moves through the wind, several things will happen or will need to be done:

1) The jib will back and will fill with wind, but because its clew is still held by the starboard jib sheet it will pivot the boat downwind to port.

2) To counter the backed jib's pivoting action the helm must be completely reversed; in this example, the helm is moved to port.

3) During 2 above the main sheet can be fully released, allowing this sail to feather downwind.

The yacht will take time to settle down because the jib and tiller are operating in opposition: the jib is pivoting the yacht downwind, but it is also driving it through the water. Thus as the yacht picks up speed the tiller will 'bite', turning the boat up into the wind; the jib will therefore lose its drive and the boat will slow; the tiller now loses its bite and the jib will once again pivot the yacht downwind... At this point the boat should be 'scalloping across the wind' at some 60 degrees and making under one knot. The tiller may be lashed down, though in such a way that it can be released instantly.

To recover from a hove-to position, wait until the backed jib is moving the boat through the water, then release the backing jib sheet and haul in the other jib sheet. At the same time, release the tiller and haul in the main.

2

CHARTS

There are so many things essential to the safe passage of a yacht that it is almost impossible to single out any one as the most important piece of sea-going equipment. However, the yachtsman who left a berth without an adequate set of good quality, up-to-date charts for the area in which the yacht will sail could be in serious trouble; likewise appropriate plotting instruments and the knowledge of how to use them are also essential. Moreover it is worth bearing in mind that nowadays, any incident involving inadequate equipment could quite possibly lead to legal proceedings.

At the time of writing, Admiralty, Imray and Stanford are just three examples of marine chart suppliers; electronic chart plotters are also increasingly available and are superb to use. First, however, we will discuss the traditional paper chart, namely that flat representation of some named part of our spherical earth's surface. The problem here is that in projecting any part of a sphere's surface onto a flat surface, some distortion is caused, and this problem is exacerbated in chart projections because the earth is not even a true sphere, the distance between the poles being smaller than its diameter at the equator. In fact it is not even a true spheroid because the surface is uneven, so that calculating the centre of the earth from different points on its surface produces different answers. The upshot to all this is that cartographers around the world produce slightly different co-ordinates of latitude and longitude.

Until recently, UK charts have been based on a lat./long. grid reference called the 'Ordnance Survey Great Britain 1936' (OSGB36), which differs from the European chart datum of 1950. Originally these differences were of no interest to the practical yachtsman, since when on passage, transfers from one chart to another were usually done long before landfall was reached when such differences are insignificant, and inshore navigation was completed using one particular reference. However, satellite navigation (GPS) has introduced a third reference: the 'World Geodetic System 1984' (WGS84). The difference between these three references can be several hundred metres, so that inshore navigators transferring a GPS-derived position onto a paper chart of a different reference may well be sailing into danger.

New paper charts will either carry 'correcting data' for the navigator to read and use, or they will be based on the satellite reference of WGS84. It is also important to realize that GPS has been deliberately degraded for civilian use, with the result that errors of 100m (330ft) and in extreme cases 300m (980ft) can be experienced; couple this with the error due to a different chart reference, and who knows where you might be – certainly the on-board navigator doesn't. It is perhaps worth mentioning again that, wonderful though electronic navigational aids may be, they are, and must always be regarded as, just aids. Given that the navigator transfers a GPS position onto a paper chart, certain checks should always be carried out; for instance: does the echo-sounder reading agree with the charted depth? How far off your EP is the GPS position? If there is a substantial difference, and your EP was worked up from a good 'land fix' taken only a couple of hours before, then the accuracy of the GPS position must be at least suspect. Under such circumstances, especially when running along a coast in dirty weather, proceed with caution and make every endeavour to fix your position. This is all very easy for me to say when sitting at a keyboard – however, I merely want to emphasize that a GPS-derived position is not infallible.

The UK Hydrographic Office is the official distributor for Admiralty charts and publications, and these are probably the most accurate source of information available to the yachtsman. *The Home Waters Catalogue* (NP109) lists and graphically illustrates the charts available; in particular it marks those available as 'small craft' editions produced in folded format, and those for the new electronic Raster Chart Service. The catalogue also details other publications, such as:

Admiralty List of Lights
Admiralty List of Radio Signals
Admiralty Sailing Directions (Pilots)
Admiralty Notices to Mariners
Tidal Stream Atlases
Tidal Publications

Admiralty charts are purchased from appointed distributors, listed in the catalogue.

As far as possible Admiralty charts are corrected to the date of purchase; from that time on it is the mariner's responsibility to maintain the integrity of the chart using the weekly *Admiralty Notices to Mariners* – these are now available in both paper and digital form. Small craft editions of these notices are available four times a year.

Chart Scales

Charts are produced to a wide range of scales. For example, the scale of chart number 3725 (Baltimore harbour) is 1:6250, while chart number 2, covering the UK, Shetland and Orkney Islands, Ireland and part of the French coast, is 1:1,500,000. Somewhat confusingly the scale 1:6250 is referred to as a 'large scale', perhaps because 1/6250 is a much larger value than 1/1,500,000. The scale 1:6250 certainly gives much greater detail than the 1:1,500,000 scale, and is used in harbour plans – as in chart 3725 – where such detail is necessary.

When planning a passage, large-scale charts of departure and destination ports are required. It is also highly desirable to have large-scale plans of intermediate ports in case you need to run for one of these in bad weather, or some accident makes it necessary to curtail the trip. A smaller-scale chart encompassing both the point of departure and the destination provides the navigator with an overall view of the whole journey and enables him to lay off a ground track from start to finish, when any dangers will be immediately obvious. It should be borne in mind that if the passage is a long one, a single 'passage chart' may, because of its small scale, omit some detail, in which case several 'medium-scale' passage plans may be a safer bet.

Chart Projections

A chart projection is a method of representing some named part of the globe's curved surface onto a flat paper chart. Several different projection methods are used, but each one introduces some distortion in the transfer. The three most common to the marine chart industry are the Mercator projection; the transverse Mercator projection; and the gnomic projection.

The Mercator Projection

First published in 1569, Mercator's projection allows the navigator to plot his course as a straight line from start to finish of the yacht's passage. The chart is constructed so that:

1) a yacht's straight course, technically a rhumb line, cuts all meridians at the same angle;
2) angles between rhumb lines are true as between earth and chart;
3) the equator, a rhumb line, appears as a straight line;
4) parallels of latitude, rhumb lines all, appear as straight lines;

5) meridians appear as straight, equi-distant lines at right-angles to the equator.

This last feature introduces one of the two inherent distortions of Mercator: since actual meridians converge at the poles, the linear distance on the earth's surface between two meridians decreases with increased latitude; thus on Mercator, land masses at high latitudes are shown as being much wider than they really are.

The nautical mile is 1,850m (2,023 yards) long, and so it is very nearly equal to one minute of latitude, or one minute of any great circle of the earth. For all practical purposes the latitude scale on a Mercator chart is therefore used directly as a measure of nautical distance; the longitude scale, for the reasons discussed above, is only ever used to measure angular differences of longitude. Also, the concept of parallel meridians breaks down completely at the poles, and some other method of projection must be employed in that area, as we shall see later.

The Mercator projection is described as a 'cylindrical orthomorphic projection', and it is often represented, incorrectly, as a world placed inside a cylinder, with meridians and parallels of latitude extended to the surface of the cylinder; when the cylinder is unwrapped the graticules of latitude and longitude are seen as described above. Fig. 12 shows this analogy and illustrates the second inherent distortion of Mercator, which is that the linear distance between parallels of latitude on a Mercator chart increases with increased latitude.

In truth, Mercator is a mathematically derived projection: on any one Mercator chart the parallels of latitude are shown as straight lines of finite length, and the meridians as straight lines perpendicular to them; the longitude scale is therefore fixed by that finite length for all lines of latitude on that chart. For item 2 above to be true, the scale for latitude at any point must increase with latitude. For the mathematically advantaged, the scale of latitude and distance at any point is proportional to the secant of the latitude at that point. All this means in practice is that the mariner using a Mercator chart can lay off a course as a straight line of length equal to the distance run, the bearing of the line being equal to the course steered.

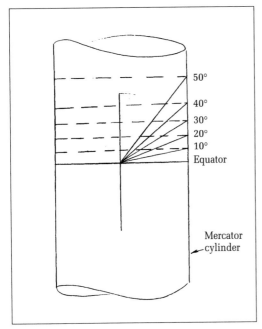

Fig 12 The 'Mercator cylinder' enclosing the globe of the earth, in the Mercator projection the 'angles of latitude' are extended to the cylinder walls to form the Mercator parallels of latitude. Notice the non linearity of the scale, the charted distance between the parallel lines of latitude increases with increasing latitude.

Meridians of longitude are also extended to the cylinder, in doing so the lines of longitude are represented as equidistant parallel lines.

The distortions inherent in Mercator charts are insignificantly small to the UK/European mariner, since the distances involved are too short for the error to be noticeable, being less than the thickness of a pencil line.

Great Circle Sailing

Plotting a course on a Mercator chart is rhumb line sailing, in which a constant course is maintained. Imagine, if you will, a yacht crossing the equator steering 045°T. If this course is maintained, and if we removed all those areas of land onto which our imaginary yacht would flounder, where would the yacht end its passage? The answer would be, at the North Pole! Remember that a rhumb line cuts all meridians at the same angle, here 45°, so that as the meridians curve over the earth's surface, converging as they do towards the poles, our yacht would be propelled towards an icy doom.

To make the shortest passage between two points on the earth's surface a yacht's course must be on the arc of a great circle (a great circle is one which bisects the earth, that is, its plane passes through the centre of the earth). Please now imagine a second yacht crossing the equator at 045°T but this time on a great circle course – it is to circle our 'landless' globe and come back to its present position. What will the yacht's course be 1) at its most northerly point? 2) as it crosses the equator, on the other side of the world? 3) at its most southerly point? The answers are 1) 090°; 2) 135°; 3) 090° (see Fig. 13).

The problem with great circle sailing is that a constant alteration of course is required throughout the passage in order to stay on the great circle, and this is

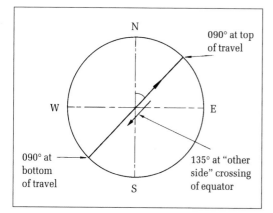

Fig. 13 Great circle sailing.

clearly not practical. So, how to solve this apparent dilemma?

The Gnomic Projection

Using this projection, any straight line plotted onto a chart is a great circle. The gnomic chart is produced by projecting the surface of the earth as seen from its centre onto the tangent plane at any convenient point. Fig. 14 illustrates this method and shows the resultant graticules of latitude and longitude; from it you will also see that any great circle projected onto the chart will be a straight line. Unfortunately this method of projection produces distortion of both latitude and longitude scales, so it is not feasible to lay off-course distances, angles of courses or bearings.

A long distance, great circle sailing course – that is, one of greater than 600 nautical miles – is plotted on a gnomic chart, from departure point to destination, as a straight line. The plotted line is 'true' in the sense that it cuts through every point of latitude and longitude that the vessel will pass through on its passage. In practice the great circle track is

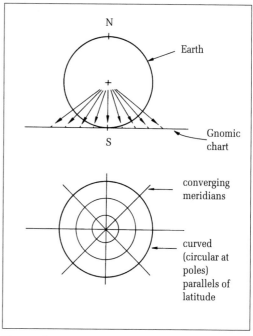

Fig. 14 The gnomic projection.

divided into suitable sailing lengths, and the latitude and longitude of each point is transferred to a Mercator chart to produce a succession of rhumb lines. This type of sailing is often referred to as approximate great circle sailing, and it means that the vessel would change course at each rhumb line.

Transverse Mercator Projection

This method of producing charts is to wrap a flat sheet around the globe touching both poles; remember the 'normal Mercator' wrapped sheet touches the globe at the equator. Transverse projection produces curved meridians of longitude and curved lines of latitude; however, since it is only used to produce large-scale charts and harbour plans, the errors are insignificant to the yachtsman and rhumb line plotting can be used. You will, however, find a nautical mileage scale printed on such charts.

Chart Titles

All charts are identified by name, indicating the area covered, and by a unique identification number – for example Rye Harbour 1991. The title area on a chart also includes the following information:

1) the scale used for the area covered, for example 1:150,000;
2) depths, measured in metres and reduced to LAT (the 'lowest astronomical tide': see below);
3) heights; drying heights are underlined and annotated in metres and decimetres measured above LAT; all other heights are measured above MHWS;
4) the projection used; until recently this was based on OSGB36, but it may now be based on WGS72 for compatibility with positions obtained using GPS;
5) authorities.

Other text information may include notes on wrecks, satellite-derived position corrections, power cables and traffic separation schemes.

The chart itself is a massive encyclopedia of navigational information, the most important being perhaps the least depth of water at any point. Every depth shown on a chart is referred to as a 'sounding', namely the depth of water remaining at the time of the lowest possible predicted tide at that point; such a tide is called the 'lowest astronomical tide', or LAT. However, just a warning about soundings: it may be a good idea to find out when the sounding was made, and if there has been any silting since that time...

Modern charts are colour-coded: white areas indicate water of a depth which, depending on the chart scale, is greater than 10 or 20m; shallower areas 10 to 5m (20 to 10) are light blue; and soundings of 5 to 0m (10 to 0) are darker blue. Drying heights – those areas which show above the water at some states of some tides – are coloured green; such areas also have individual figures in the form $\underline{Xy}$ – for example $\underline{3}_4$ indicates an area of height 3.4m above LAT. The land is yellow.

Depth contours – that is, lines on the chart joining equal depths – may identify 0, 2, 5, 10, 15, 20 etc metre soundings, and are very useful to the mariner taking a passage along a shore in fog. You will also notice that depth contours are drawn round isolated seabed 'hills and hollows'; these individual changes in depth can be very dramatic and are therefore identifiable on the echo sounder, confirming or otherwise an EP. Note, too, that changes in soundings off headlands can be super-dramatic: due to the change in sea levels over the centuries, land which was once part of an extending headland is now submerged, and due to erosion, forms a ridge on the seabed; this may offer a sudden mountain-like obstruction to tidal flows, and in order to pass over it the water will rise abruptly, causing what are politely called 'confused seas' or 'races'. In cases of a severe race hazard a chart warning symbol is printed in the area and the wise yachtsman will take heed of it. A really confused sea area will throw a yacht around uncontrollably, steering will be almost impossible, and the boom may well be backed across the cockpit.

Rocks and navigation marks on the north Brittany coast.

Conspicuous Land Structures

Features on shore such as church spires, water towers, hotels and flagpoles are shown, sometimes marked 'conspic'. Three-point fixes rely on such items, and as we shall see, a 'good fix' is a heart-warming position to plot. The mariner must of course ensure that the actual shore features used to get the three bearings are the same charted features used on the chart plot.

Navigational Aids

Buoyage, lighthouses and lights are covered in Chapter 8.

Traffic Separation Schemes (TSS)

In certain sea areas commercial traffic density is so great that ships must make passage using well defined sea lanes, rather as cars must keep to their own side of the roadway; such lanes are well marked, with thick magenta-coloured lines on the relevant charts. They are monitored by the authorities and the regulation is strictly enforced. Small boats are not allowed into a TSS except when it is necessary to cross them, for instance in certain parts of the Channel when on passage from the UK to France, and such crossing must be made giving the largest visual and radar aspect possible, that is, with the yacht's heading at right-angles to the general direction of the TSS.

Charts within Charts

At the limit(s) of the sea area(s) covered by a chart the identifying number of any adjoining chart(s) is (are) given; also if a larger scale chart exists for any given area on a particular chart, the area of that chart is outlined in magenta and its number printed within the outline.

Compass Roses

The detail of a compass rose will be dealt with later; suffice it to say here that at least one compass rose, and more often two or three, will be shown on a chart giving both true and magnetic values, with details of magnetic variation appended. It is interesting to note that the value of magnetic variation changes over quite small distances.

Tidal Levels and Streams

Tides and tidal streams will be covered in detail in a later chapter; however, charts do list the heights of mean high and low waters for areas of significance on the chart, together with the latitude and longitude of those places. This list allows the mariner a quick reference to depths without referring to a tidal almanac. A table of tide streams giving set and drift figures for named locations on the chart are referenced to time of high water at some standard port such as Dover.

Chart Corrections

New charts and new versions of existing charts are sold as up to date as the latest information available to the Hydrographic Department. Subsequent to purchase, all charts should be corrected by the owner using the information in the *Notices to Mariners* published weekly, or in the quarterly *Small Craft Notices*.

It should be noted that where a vessel is in an accident involving navigational error, the chart in use at the time may be examined by the appropriate authority, and the other party's lawyer.

The date of a chart's edition is printed in the bottom right-hand margin; this should be confirmed as the latest edition by reference to the current NP234, the cumulative list of *Admiralty Notices to Mariners*, a Hydrographic Department's publication which lists the current edition of all charts and subsequent Ns to Ms. Corrections made by the owner should be noted at the bottom left margin of the chart.

Chart Bearings and Courses

The direction of a yacht's course and all bearings plotted on a Mercator chart are measured in degrees true, ie from the geographic north pole in a clockwise direction, using three-figure notation:

true north = 000°
due east   = 090°
due south = 180°
due west   = 270°

Fig. 15 shows a compass rose with an outer circle in degrees true and an inner circle marked off in degrees magnetic; more about the magnetic circle later.

A second method of defining a direction is the system of 'points of the compass' in which each of the four cardinal points – north, south, east and west – is subdivided into eight points, each of 11¼° and named. For example in the quadrant north to east the points are:

N, NbyE, NNE, NEbyN, NE, NEbyE, ENE, EbyN, E.

A full picture of the points system is shown at Fig. 16. This system is still used in weather forecasting for wind direc-

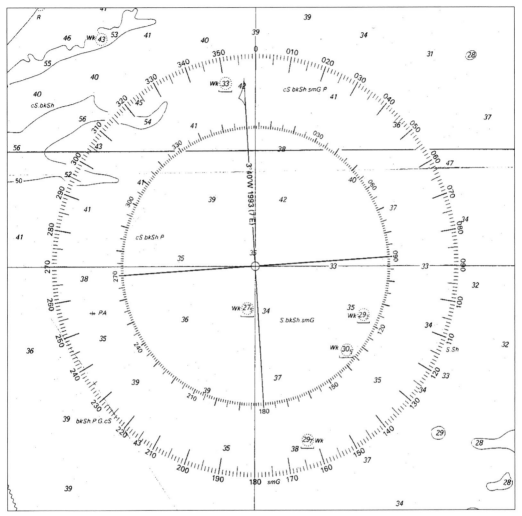

Fig 15 The compass rose.

tion, and is therefore useful knowledge. To recite in succession the points of the compass is said to be 'boxing the compass'.

Chart Instruments

For chartwork the mariner should use the following:

1. A soft 2B pencil and a soft rubber; charts are expensive and need treating carefully. Every line you plot will eventually have to be gently erased, so lines should be only as long as necessary and not heavily drawn.

2. A pair of brass dividers; these are specially made for distance measurement when plotting on the chart and can be used with one hand.

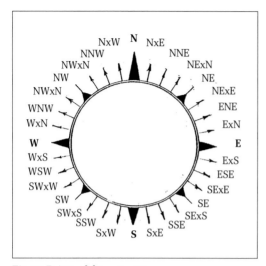

Fig. 16 Points of the compass.

3. One of the following: parallel ruler, Breton plotter, rolling ruler, Douglas protractor or Hurst plotter. There is no 'best instrument', and every user has his or her favourite. My choice is a pair of parallel rules with angle gradations around the periphery, the advantage of having the peripheral angle scale being that any meridian or vertical straight line on the chart can be used to set the bearing or course to be plotted. This greatly limits the need to 'work' the parallel rule across the chart, thus minimizing the chances of having to start again in the event of slipping or encountering 'something' under the chart.

Chart 5011

This is actually a booklet, which illustrates and has examples of every special feature that may appear on your chart. Fig. 17 shows just a few examples of how these special features are indicated.

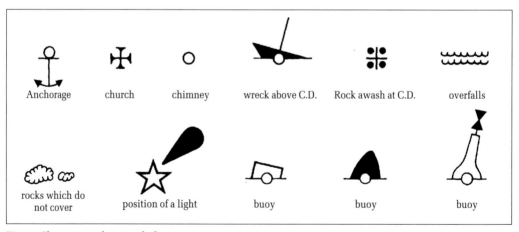

Fig. 17 Chart 5011- chart symbols.

3

THE MAGNETIC COMPASS

The chart, the magnetic compass and the 'distance run' log are the three basic instruments enabling the mariner to make a safe passage across the seaways and oceans of the world. The magnetic, or perhaps now the electronic compass in association with the chart and log ensure that a calculated, known and safe passage can be made from departure point to destination.

On a chart, the meridians of longitude converge on remote geographical north and south poles; the outer circle of the compass rose has the true bearing 000°(T) aligned to the remote geographical north pole, and all true bearings are referenced to this alignment. Unfortunately the position of the magnetic north pole is off to one side of the true pole; this difference in position is called magnetic variation (see below) and must be taken into account when transferring a 'true' course or bearing from the chart to the magnetic compass.

Magnetic Variation

In European waters the magnetic pole is offset west from the true pole by some 3°; it moves slowly eastwards at some 7' to 10' of arc annually. This means that a magnetic compass in UK waters will read some 3° higher than the true bearing: the difference is called magnetic variation. Since at any one time the magnetic pole is situated some few degrees away from the true pole, a study of Fig. 18 will show that the value of magnetic variation is position-dependent and will be zero at two particular opposite meridians.

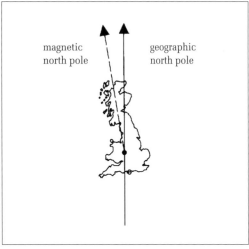

magnetic north pole

geographic north pole

Fig 18 When seen from the UK. The magnetic pole is approximately 3°W of the true pole. When seen from the opposite side of the world (longitude 180°) the magnetic pole would be some 3°E of the true pole.

Variation, due entirely to the misalignment of the geographic and magnetic poles, is the reason that the inner, magnetic circle on a charted compass rose is offset, as shown at Fig. 15. Note also from this figure that the value of variation is specified for a particular year and annotated with its annual change: for example 3° 40'W 1989 (10'E) means that in this position the magnetic pole was 3° 40' west of the true pole in 1989 and has been moving east, that is, decreasing by 10' annually from that time.

Magnetic Deviation

Magnetic deviation describes a second compass error: namely, it is the effect upon a yacht's compass of local magnetic effects and the presence of ferrous materials on board the yacht itself. The inboard engine, electrical circuitry and iron ballast keels are just some of the items that will permanently pull the magnetic compass away from the magnetic pole. Also, try to avoid leaving tools or any other metal items in the vicinity of the compass, even temporarily, since they will inevitably pull it one way or the other.

Deviation changes according to the yacht's heading; thus it may well pull the compass off to the east on one heading, to the west on a second, and have no effect on a third. Fortunately the deviation for each yacht can be measured and in most cases reduced to an insignificantly small value.

Total Compass Error

The total compass error is the algebraic sum of variation and deviation: if both errors are named east, or if both are named west, simply add them together and name the total error east or west respectively. But if the errors are named differently, then subtract the smaller from the larger and name the result after the larger of the two.

Example 1: If variation is 4°W and deviation is 2°W, the total error is 6°W. This means that a compass bearing or course would read 6° bigger than the true bearing or course.

Example 2: If variation is 3°W and deviation 5°E, the total compass error would be (5°–3°)E = 2°E. The compass course would therefore read 2° lower than the true course.

Please complete the following exercises before leaving this section:

1. Assuming that variation is 5°W, calculate the true course given the following data:

a. Compass course 040(°C) deviation 1°W
b. Compass course 165(°C) deviation 3°E
c. Compass course 245(°C) deviation 2°E

2. Assuming 5°W variation, find the compass course:

a. True course 036(°T) deviation 2°W
b. True course 124(°T) deviation 7°E
c. True course 158(°T) deviation 2°E

The answers are:

1) 034°T, 163°T, 242°T
2) 043°C, 122°C, 161°C

The Deviation Card

Where a vessel's deviation cannot be reduced to zero, a deviation card is produced by the compass adjuster; the card quite literally plots the value of deviation against the ship's heading, as shown at Fig. 19. The measured value of deviation is shown for each 45° of ship's heading. Notice that the curve swings east and west of zero: for example, on a ship's heading of 090° the deviation is approximately 4°E, indicating that the compass is being pulled 4° east of the magnetic pole, whilst a heading of 315° produces a 6° west deviation.

The skipper should check the deviation of the yacht's main compass periodically; there are two popular ways of measuring deviation whilst on passage:

1. By using the hand-bearing compass to check the course being steered by the main compass: stand in the forepart of the yacht, as far as possible away from any magnetic effects, and the difference between the two compass readings must be the deviation on that heading. Where the hand-bearing compass is greater, the deviation must be east.

2. By heading along a charted transit where the transit bearing is given on the chart, or making up your own transit line(s) from conspicuous shore objects, and checking your course as you steer along it. The problem with this method is tidal effect, because if any tide is running – and generally there will be a tidal set and drift – the yacht will be heading upstream to maintain the transit: that is, the ship's heading is not along the transit course.

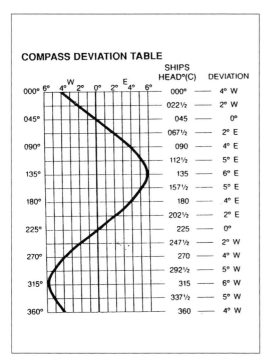

COMPASS DEVIATION TABLE

SHIPS HEAD°(C)	DEVIATION
000°	4° W
022½	2° W
045	0°
067½	2° E
090	4° E
112½	5° E
135	6° E
157½	5° E
180	4° E
202½	2° E
225	0°
247½	2° W
270	4° W
292½	5° W
315	6° W
337½	5° W
360	4° W

Fig. 19 The deviation card.

Swinging the Compass: the Pelorus

A compass is swung by taking bearings from a known charted position, of an object 5 miles (8km) or more away, using a pelorus. The latter can be made up from a flat square of ply to which is glued a compass rose and a centre-pivoted wood pointer with two sighting nails; it is placed on the coachroof with its 000°T mark aligned with the fore-and-aft line of the yacht. To swing the compass the yacht is either moored in a known position, in such a way that she can be hauled round onto various headings, or she is steered closely round a known beacon, while relative bearings of the distant object are taken. The table below illustrates the necessary reading to be taken.

Ship's heading *compass*	Pelorus bearing *object*	Compass bearing *object*	Charted bearing *mag.*	Deviation
000	150	150	151	1°E
030	119	149	151	2°E
060	090	150	151	1°E
090	061	151	151	0°

In the above table the error of deviation, if any, lies hidden in the data of the first column. Where deviation is zero, the sum of the first two columns – that is, the data of column three – should equal the magnetic charted bearing shown in column four. Where the data of columns three and four differ, the difference is the compass deviation on that bearing. Further, when column three data is smaller than column four, the deviation is east.

A ship's course or a bearing can be quoted in degrees true, degrees magnetic or degrees compass:

1. A course in degrees true, referenced from the geographic north pole, is abbreviated °T.
2. A course in degrees magnetic, referenced from the magnetic pole ie allowing for variation, is abbreviated °M.
3. A course in degrees compass, referenced from the compass pole ie allowing for variation and deviation, is abbreviated °C.

Since there can be a considerable difference in the value of these referenced courses, it is important that all on board know where to use them. For instance, when a course line or bearing is drawn on a chart and annotated, the convention is to use the true figure: this means that the °T is optional and may be omitted. In consequence, if a navigator or watch leader insists on annotating the course line using the value obtained for either 2 or 3 above, it is essential that the appropriate °M or °C is printed against the value written on the chart.

Finally, here are two little odes on this subject:

1. Total error west, compass best.
Meaning, if the total compass error is west, the compass reading will be bigger than the true one.
2. Total error east, compass least.
Meaning, if the total compass error is east, the compass reading will be smaller than the true one.

Heeling Error

The effect of deviation on a magnetic compass changes as the yacht's course changes because the relative position of the compass needle and the ferrous material causing the deviation has itself changed. Similarly, when a yacht is heeled over such that her lee rail is awash, the error-causing ferrous material will have swung to a new relative position and this change may affect the value of deviation. Such effects are usually very small, but checks should be made.

The Electronic Compass

The electromagnetic fluxgate compass exploits the science of electromagnetic induction in which a current-carrying coil of wire (called the primary winding), wrapped around a suitable core, will magnetize that core, thereby forming an electro-magnet, one end of the core becoming a north magnetic pole, the other a south pole. When the current in the primary is an alternating one, the direction of induced magnetism in the core will reverse as the current reverses, and under such circumstances an alternating voltage will be induced into any secondary coil wrapped around the same core.

If two identical primary coils are used, wound in opposite directions around the core, the electro-magnetizing forces in the core are cancelled, and the induced current in the secondary winding falls to zero. External magnetic fields such as that of the earth upset this balance so that an induced voltage exists in the secondary winding, and can be measured.

In the fluxgate compass several such elements are arranged in a ring, and by comparing the induced voltages around this ring the direction of the earth's magnetic pole can be deduced: thus we have a 'no moving parts' electronic compass. Other advantages are the ease of connection to on-board electronic navigation instruments; and the fact that reading(s) can be stored for later retrieval – very handy for three-point fixes.

In use the compass must be horizontal otherwise large errors can be generated.

4

CHARTWORK 1

We have so far discussed the chart as a source of navigational data, and the magnetic compass. The chart provides us with all the necessary information about our surroundings, the depth of water, navigational hazards and safe transit lines; now we shall see that it allows the navigator to construct a safe sea passage or 'ground track' from departure to destination. The magnetic compass – its course corrected for variation and deviation – allows the helm to steer along the navigator's charted true course. Our third basic aid is the ship's 'distance' log, which enables the mariner to measure the distance run through the water and hence calculate the speed of his yacht through the water.

The Log

The log is either an analogue taffrail/Walker log or an electronic one. The Walker log comprises a mechanical counter with an analogue dial mounted on a special bracket at the stern of the boat; the counter is driven by a propeller trailed behind the yacht at the end of a long cord – when the boat moves through the water the propeller spins and the cord

transmits the spin to the counter. Note that the recovery of the Walker's propeller after use needs to be done in a particular way: when pulling in the long trailing cord, allow the recovered part of it to fall back into the water until the propeller is on board, and only then retrieve it – in this way the rotating propeller will not snare up the cord during the recovery operation.

An electronic log consists of an under-hull transducer which may be entirely electromagnetic, or it may have an external impeller with a digital dial fitted at the navigator's position in the cabin and probably a repeater dial in the cockpit. The electronic log is most convenient since all we have to do is switch it on and read the dial. However, if the log is of the type with a hull-fitted impeller, periodically this will need to be cleaned. In order to do this the transducer is removed from its hull-piercing fitting in the bilge, and immediately a substitute bung is placed into the transducer fitting to halt the inrush of water. This action of momentarily but deliberately allowing sea water to rush into the bilges is not as fearful as it may seem; study the dummy plug before you start and carry out the operation smartly – the actual amount of sea water entering the boat will be quite small. When cleaned of any marine debris the process is reversed and the transducer refitted.

Several days before any sea passage the skipper will have planned at least the outline of the trip, collecting information on such things as the weather and the tides; he will have spent time:

1) Watching and listening to weather forecasts to see what the wind strengths and directions are likely to be; he may also have obtained a fax for the next three days of weather from 'Marine Call' – these reports give both text and weather plots and are extremely useful.

2) Observing the phase of the moon; this will inform him of spring or neap tides, and reference to tidal almanacs will give times of high and low water.

The more planning you do before arriving at the boat, the quicker you can 'let go' and enjoy sailing.

Plotting a Position

Good chartwork, accurately and neatly performed, is the hallmark of good and safe seamanship. A yacht's position is only accurately known when the yacht is berthed in a good harbour; at any other time its position is suspect. As we shall see, a mariner strives constantly to calculate and plot his position, and knowing how to 'read' a chart, plot his course, use compass and log, and estimate for tide and wind, are all necessary skills that allow the yacht's position to be estimated during the passage.

On any passage the first pieces of information to be noted are the latitude and

longitude of the departure point, the time of departure and the log reading, all should be recorded and marked on the chart. In this day and age electronic navigation instruments can be used side by side with traditional methods of position fixing, and it is wise to note that even the manufacturers of such equipment emphasize that their instruments are an aid only – undoubtedly wonderful, but even so, a prudent skipper will keep his paper and pencil chart and narrative log up to date.

Leaving a harbour or a well marked channel, the departure point is easily recognized on the chart and a 'fix' plotted – at, for example, two cables due south of the harbour entrance, and two cables to starboard of the fairway buoy. A charted fix is shown as a dot inside a small circle, and the fix should be annotated with the time and log reading. These should also be noted in the yacht's narrative log.

Plotting a Course: Dead Reckoning

There are many delights to be had from sailing, and one of them is pre-planning the sailing trip, especially when on the actual day of departure there is either no wind, or it is too strong, or it is coming from the wrong direction. Such differences between expectation and actuality are to be anticipated, however, and merely mean having to modify the sailing plan. On the day this begins with a check on the overall passage chart, which encompasses departure and expected arrival point, or at least the first leg of the passage, to ensure that the 'ground track' is safe. The ground track is that line plotted on the chart along which the yacht is intended to pass over, and shallows, rocks and overfalls – in fact all navigational danger points – should be a good half mile off this line. Navigational aids such as buoys, lighthouses, transits, conspic(uous) shore items, should all be noted for use on the passage. The ground track plotted on the chart is marked with a double arrow.

With the ground track plotted, sails are hoisted and the course set. One hour later the navigator reads the log and asks the helm for the course steered over this period. Subtracting the value of the log at the time of departure from its current reading reveals the distance travelled, through the water, along our course. Asking the helm what course has been steered will reveal any errors or bias to port or starboard of the course intended. The distance travelled is marked off with a short crossing line on the ground track, and annotated with ship's time and log. To avoid possible confusion the log value is printed in a 'long-footed L'. Fig. 20 shows a ground track of 5 nautical miles (n.m.) on a course of 060°T, annotated with time and log readings.

In the above example we used only compass course steered and distance run to calculate our position after one hour's sailing. This 'dead reckoning' (DR) position is the least amount of chartwork that must be done, every hour, at every course change and every watch change – as we shall see, a DR position is not the most accurate way of calculating a vessel's position.

We assumed in the above one hour DR plot that the tidal flow was zero. This is only rarely true, however, so let us now assume that a 2-knot tidal stream will be with us – ie favourable for half the journey – and a 3-knot foul tide – ie against us

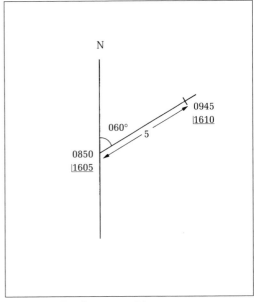

Fig. 20 Dead reckoning position.

– for the second half. In the first half hour our sails will push us 2.5 n.m. 'through the water', and the water itself will have moved 1.0 n.m. over the ground in our direction, a total forward journey of 2.5 + 1.0 = 3.5 n.m. over the ground.

In the second half hour, our sails will push us 2.5 n.m. through the water, but the water will have moved backwards over the ground, carrying us with it, a distance of 1.5 n.m.; thus our total forward distance will be 2.5 – 1.5 = 1 n.m. At the end of our first hour therefore our position will be 4.5 n.m. from our starting position along the ground track – though please note that we cannot call this position a DR since its construction took account of more than just compass and log. (Later we will take into account those times when a tidal stream will be flowing at some angle to the boat's heading other than from right ahead or astern.)

Three-Point Fix

A vessel's position can be accurately plotted on the chart by taking the bearing of three known – that is, charted – shore features or buildings. The bearings are taken with a hand-bearing compass, and each when plotted gives a 'position line', so called because the yacht's position must be somewhere on each one of the lines. The three plotted position lines must cross at one point, and this point fixes the position of the yacht at the time the bearings were taken.

In practice the three position lines will rarely cross at a single point, but over a small triangular area called a 'cocked hat'. This positional discrepancy usually occurs because of the difficulty in taking bearings from a platform which is moving simultaneously in all three dimensions. A three-point fix is shown at Fig. 21; the figure also shows significant points to note when using a hand-bearing compass:

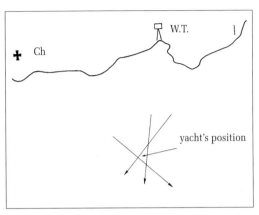

Fig. 21 The three-point fix.

1. Shore objects whose bearings are being taken should be not further than three miles distant.

2. Shore objects whose bearings are being taken should be approximately 30° apart.

3. Bearings on, or near, the beam should be taken last

5

TIDES

The tidal rise and fall of the world's oceans is caused by the gravitational forces between the earth, the moon and the sun. Each day as the earth rotates on its axis, the waters of the earth immediately below the moon and those on the opposite side of the earth are physically lifted – that is, a 'high water' level develops in these two places. And since the volume of the earth's water is finite, there is a corresponding 'low water' level at the two midway points. The high water level 'follows' the orbit of the moon, with a slight delay due to friction, in its apparently diurnal journey around the world. Theoretically there should be two high and two low waters in every 24-hour period of the earth's rotation. However, as we shall see, things are not that simple.

Lunar Tides

It is clear from the table below that the relative diameters of the sun and moon, and their distance from the earth, are hugely different; but although the sun is much, much bigger than the moon, its greater distance away in effect reduces its enormous size so that it acts as no more than a modifier of the lunar tidal highs and lows. We shall see later exactly what this modification is.

Diameter	Distance
Moon: 2,160 miles (3,475km)	24,000 miles (38,616km)
Sun: 864,000 miles (1,390,176km)	93,000,000 miles (149,637,000km)

As we have discussed briefly above, the earth's daily spin should generate two high and low water levels; however, that is not the full story, and we must consider now the effect of the moon's orbit around the earth. This takes 27.3 days, and during each 24-hour earth spin the moon moves a small distance along its orbit – in fact it will have moved 1/27.3 of its orbit each day. In theory therefore the earth would have to turn a little further on its axis for high waters to occur at the same place on its surface as on the previous day – in practice it means that the times of high and low water occur a little later each day, the approximate diurnal delay being given by the formula:

$$24/27.3 = 52 \text{ minutes}$$

Theoretically during every 24 hour and 50 minute period there will be two high and two low waters, each high water occurring 12 hours and 25 minutes after the previous one. However, friction against the ocean floor and resistance from continental shelves, together with underwater interferences and obstacles, all lead to a wide variety of tidal behaviour around the world. In European waters semi-diurnal tides are most common, that is, the theoretical two high and two low waters in each 24 hour and 50 minute period. Other parts of the globe have just one high and one low water each day, some coasts have 12m (40ft) tides, while others, such as in the Mediterranean, rise and fall by only a few centimetres.

Solar Tides

The modifying effect of the sun's gravity is most noticeable on two specific occasions:

1) When the sun, the moon and the earth are in line, the combined gravitation of sun and moon giving rise to the highest of high water levels and the lowest of low water levels. This occurs twice during each lunar orbit, when the moon is in line between the earth and sun, and when the earth is in line between the moon and sun. Such tides are called 'spring tides', and they happen approximately every two weeks.

2) When the sun and moon are at right angles to one another, or in space quadrature. At these two periods in the moon's orbit the individual gravities are pulling at 90° to each other, resulting in the lowest of high water levels and the highest of low water levels. These tides are called 'neap tides', and they also occur every two weeks, between the spring tides.

The Phases of the Moon

When the moon is in line with the sun, and between the earth and the sun, it is said to be a 'new' moon, and since an earth-bound observer would be looking at a completely unlit hemisphere of the moon, it should be invisible against the dark sky; however, the new moon is most often seen as a crescent shape. At this point the earth will be experiencing spring tides. Over the following seven nights or so the crescent is seen to 'fill' as the moon completes approximately one quarter of its orbit. This is the time of neap tides, when sun and moon are at right angles. During the next seven nights, more and more of the moon is seen as it fills completely to become the 'round disk' of a full moon – that is, sun and moon in line again, but this time with the moon and sun on opposite sides of the earth. The observed hemisphere of the moon is fully lit, and again we have spring tides. During the next fourteen nights the moon is seen to change its shape in reverse order to its filling, to become new once again.

We know from the above that the moon takes approximately 27.3 days to orbit the earth; however, during this time the earth–moon combination will have moved a little distance along the earth's orbit of the sun, and in consequence the moon must turn a little further than its 27.3 day period to become 'in line' with the sun again – this extra turning takes 2.16 days. New moon to new moon therefore occupies some 29.5 days; it is the period of the lunar month, and is called a lunation.

Equinoxial and Solstice Tides

The earth's orbit around the sun is not of constant shape, but changes from a near-circular figure to a shallow elliptical one. It is furthest away at the solstices, when for a brief period the sun (*sol*) seems to stand (*stice*) still, on the eastern horizon as it rises from nearly the same position each day. The spring and winter solstices occur on the 21 June and 22 December respectively, and the sun's gravitational pull at this time will be at a minimum; consequently the solstice spring tides will have a smaller range than the average spring tides.

The sun is closest to the earth at the equinoxes, when the night's (*nox*) hours equal (*equi*) the daylight hours; these occur on the 21 March and the 23 September. The combined gravitational pull of the sun and the moon will have maximum effect at this time, causing the equinoxial spring and autumn tidal ranges to be greater than the average spring tide range. The changing declinations of the sun and moon also have a spring tidal effect, such that very large spring tides may occur at equinoxes.

To a sailor, the importance of the high tidal range (HW-LW) at an equinoxial spring tide is that the LW level is at, or near its absolute minimum. At times of exceptionally big equinoxial spring tide ranges the LW height may be very low indeed, and the opportunities of going aground at this time are enormous even in familiar waters – if you go aground on a really big spring, you just might be there for six months (approximately).

Tidal Height Definitions

All tidal heights are measured with respect to LAT. Some of the many definitions for the heights of the tides are shown in Fig. 22: for instance, the 'mean level' (ML) is the average depth of water at that particular place. 'Mean high water springs' (MHWS) is the average highest level of water, average because from our previous discussion of earth, moon and sun alignments it follows that some individual spring HW levels would be higher or lower than the mean. For the same reason, all the defined tidal heights shown in Fig. 22 represent a band of heights about a mean figure. 'Mean low water springs' (MLWS) defines the band of most concern to the mariner, since it is the lowest level of water that he is likely to experience and therefore the time when the greatest care must be exercised.

'Mean high water neaps' (MHWN) is the band representing the lowest of the high water periods; and 'mean low water neaps' (MLWN) the band of highest low water periods.

The 'lowest astronomical tide' (LAT), sometimes referred to as 'chart datum' (CD), is the lowest predicted level of water, and would only be reached at the low water period of the most exceptional of spring tides. Under certain meteorological conditions of extremely high-pressure air masses, the sounding may be lower than LAT.

The three most important tidal height definitions for you to know and commit to memory are these:

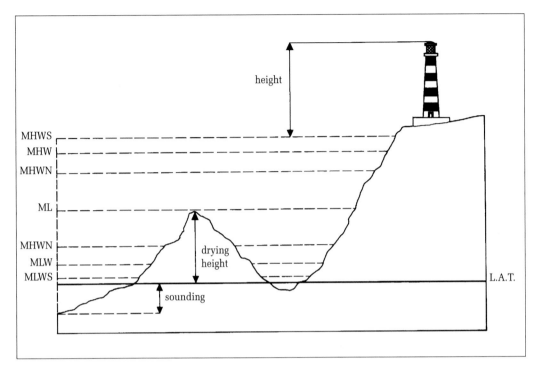

Fig. 22 Tidal heights.

(1) rise of tide: this is the height of the sea surface, at any time, above the previous/next low water; its highest value is HW-LW;

(2) height of tide: this is the sum of LW and 'rise of tide': it is literally the height of the sea level, at any time, above LAT;

(3) depth of water: this is the sum of LAT and 'height of tide'.

Soundings

Soundings are those figures found in the water areas of all charts, and identify the least depth of water at the points indicated; in normal weather conditions they are a guaranteed minimum. Fig. 22 shows areas where the seabed rises above LAT, but which may not be exposed to view by tides at MHWS or lower. Such areas are called drying heights – that is, at some states of some tides the area will show above sea level. The height of these areas above LAT is printed on the chart in the form '2_6', meaning that the height of this area is 2.6m above LAT. Land beaches are obviously drying heights as the sea shoals towards the land, but drying heights may also rise above LAT as an isolated seabed hill or rock. Such areas are to be avoided; however, you may well take the 'safe' ground in a bilge-keeled yacht, or go alongside a wall for 'below water' hull work.

The heights of overhead cables and lighthouses are also shown on charts; such measurements are taken above MHWS.

Tide Tables

The tidal heights and times for ports of the UK and associated waters are found in current copies of nautical almanacs.

Ports in the UK are listed as either standard or secondary; the latter will be dealt with later in this chapter. A standard port is usually a large commercial one with a high level of ship movement. In some of these big ports the yachtsman is provided with a 'small boat' entry and departure channel, designed specifically to keep him safely away from the big stuff. Indeed, small boats travel the main channels at their peril, and it must be remembered that large, deep-draught vessels may well be confined to the main channel with very little room for manoeuvre, and requiring long distances in which to stop. A yacht leaving Poole, for example, and venturing into the main channel on the seaward side of the chain ferry might well hear a very long, angry-sounding blast on a ship's horn, and see over his shoulder a sky-darkening towerblock, made of steel and coming up fast.

The almanac lists the time and height of high and low water of all standard ports for each day of the current year; examples are Dover and Portsmouth. Fig. 23 is a copy of the tidal predictions for the port of Portsmouth during the months of May to August; the time in GMT, and the height in metres of both high and low water for each day are listed. For example, from Fig. 23:

Friday, 12 June

Time	m
0039	1.7
0742	3.8
1304	1.5
2015	4.1

High waters occur at 0742 and 2015 GMT, the heights being 3.8m and 4.1m above LAT respectively.

Low waters occur at 0039 and 1304, the heights 1.7m and 1.5m above LAT respectively.

The range (HW-LW) of the morning tide is:
    3.8–1.7=2.1m
The range of the afternoon tide is:
    4.1–1.5=2.6m

Note that these height figures are measured above LAT: a skipper would examine the soundings on the appropriate chart and refer to the pilot to ensure the yacht's safe passage before entering. The morning LW is only 1.7m, and considering that yachts of only 27ft may well draw near this figure, even a small amount of swell would cause a grounding over areas whose LAT approaches zero.

Return to Fig. 23 again and examine the ranges of the Portsmouth tides for the period beginning 16 June. The highest range of tide occurs on the night of the 16th and the following night, when the range is 3.5m: these are spring tides, and note that the entry for the 17th is marked with a small open circle denoting the day of the full moon, ie the sun and moon are in line. Observe also that the night tide some fourteen days later on 2 July is again a spring tide, with a range of 4.1m, and that a small closed circle denoting the date of the full moon is attached to this date, too. The smallest range, the neap tide between these two dates, occurs on the morning of the 27th, being only 2.7m (4.0–1.3m). There is usually a slight delay, one to two days, between the date of a new or full moon and the associated spring tide.

TIME ZONE UT (GMT)
Summer Time add ONE hour in non-shaded area

ENGLAND, SOUTH COAST — PORTSMOUTH

Lat 50°48′ N   Long 1°07′ W

TIMES AND HEIGHTS OF HIGH AND LOW WATERS

(Times in 24-h; heights in metres, m)

MAY

Day		Tide 1	Tide 2	Tide 3	Tide 4
1	F	0147 1.2	0845 4.2	1410 0.8	2121 4.6
2	Sa	0238 0.8	0936 4.6	1501 0.5	2210 4.8
3	Su	0325 0.6	1027 4.8	1551 0.4	2259 5.0
4 ●	M	0412 0.4	1117 4.9	1640 0.3	2345 5.1
5	Tu	0459 0.3	1207 5.0	1726 0.4	
6	W	0031 5.0	0545 0.4	1256 5.0	1809 0.5
7	Th	0115 4.9	0629 0.4	1344 4.8	1851 0.8
8	F	0157 4.7	0715 0.7	1434 4.6	1936 1.1
9	Sa	0243 4.5	0804 1.0	1527 4.4	2029 1.4
10	Su	0336 4.2	0902 1.3	1618 4.0	2135 1.7
11	M	0441 3.9	1742 4.0	2256 1.8	
12	Tu	0601 3.7	1133 1.6	1901 3.9	
13	W	0019 1.8	0722 3.7	1249 1.5	2008 4.0
14	Th	0127 1.6	0828 3.9	1348 1.3	2100 4.2
15	F	0217 1.3	0918 4.0	1433 1.2	2142 4.3
16	Sa	0257 1.1	0958 4.2	1511 1.0	2218 4.5
17	Su	0331 1.0	1034 4.4	1547 1.0	2251 4.5
18	M	0405 0.9	1109 4.5	1622 0.9	2323 4.6
19	Tu	0438 0.9	1144 4.4	1657 0.9	2356 4.5
20	W	0511 0.8	1219 4.4	1729 0.9	
21	Th	0027 4.4	0542 0.8	1255 4.3	1759 1.0
22	F	0059 4.3	0615 0.9	1330 4.2	1830 1.1
23	Sa	0133 4.2	0647 0.9	1405 4.1	1904 1.2
24	Su	0209 4.1	0723 1.0	1446 4.1	1945 1.4
25	M	0251 4.0	0807 1.2	1532 4.0	2034 1.5
26	Tu	0341 3.9	0900 1.3	1629 4.0	2138 1.6
27	W	0443 3.8	1007 1.4	1736 4.0	2252 1.6
28	Th	0556 3.8	1122 1.3	1846 4.1	
29	F	0005 1.5	0706 4.0	1234 1.3	1949 4.3
30	Sa	0109 1.2	0810 4.3	1336 0.9	2047 4.6
31	Su	0206 0.9	0908 4.5	1434 0.7	2141 4.8

JUNE

Day		Tide 1	Tide 2	Tide 3	Tide 4
1	M	0259 0.7	1003 4.7	1527 0.6	2233 4.9
2 ●	Tu	0351 0.5	1058 4.8	1617 0.5	2324 5.0
3	W	0441 0.4	1151 4.9	1706 0.6	
4	Th	0011 4.9	0527 0.4	1241 4.8	1750 0.7
5	F	0056 4.8	0613 0.6	1330 4.7	1833 0.9
6	Sa	0139 4.7	0657 0.8	1418 4.6	1919 1.2
7	Su	0223 4.5	0745 1.0	1508 4.5	2010 1.4
8	M	0312 4.3	0837 1.3	1602 4.3	2109 1.7
9	Tu	0409 4.0	0938 1.5	1704 4.2	2216 1.8
10	W	0517 3.9	1046 1.6	1811 4.1	2330 1.8
11	Th	0630 3.8	1159 1.6	1917 4.0	
12	F	0039 1.7	0742 3.8	1304 1.5	2015 4.1
13	Sa	0137 1.5	0840 3.9	1357 1.4	2102 4.2
14	Su	0223 1.3	0928 4.1	1441 1.3	2143 4.3
15	M	0303 1.2	1008 4.3	1520 1.2	2220 4.4
16	Tu	0340 1.1	1046 4.3	1556 1.2	2256 4.5
17 ○	W	0415 1.0	1122 4.4	1632 1.1	2330 4.5
18	Th	0449 1.0	1157 4.3	1706 1.1	
19	F	0004 4.4	0523 0.9	1232 4.3	1740 1.1
20	Sa	0038 4.3	0557 0.9	1310 4.3	1816 1.1
21	Su	0115 4.2	0633 0.9	1350 4.3	1853 1.1
22	M	0154 4.2	0712 0.9	1434 4.3	1934 1.2
23	Tu	0238 4.1	0756 0.9	1520 4.3	2021 1.3
24	W	0326 4.1	0844 1.0	1612 4.2	2114 1.4
25	Th	0421 4.0	0942 1.1	1709 4.2	2218 1.4
26	F	0524 4.0	1048 1.2	1813 4.2	2328 1.4
27	Sa	0634 4.0	1201 1.3	1918 4.3	
28	Su	0037 1.3	0743 4.2	1309 1.2	2019 4.5
29	M	0143 1.1	0848 4.4	1411 1.0	2117 4.6
30	Tu	0242 0.9	0948 4.5	1509 0.9	2213 4.7

JULY

Day		Tide 1	Tide 2	Tide 3	Tide 4
1 ●	W	0338 0.7	1045 4.7	1602 0.8	2307 4.8
2	Th	0429 0.6	1139 4.7	1652 0.8	2357 4.7
3	F	0516 0.6	1230 4.7	1738 0.8	
4	Sa	0041 4.7	0559 0.7	1316 4.7	1820 1.0
5	Su	0123 4.6	0641 0.8	1400 4.6	1903 1.1
6	M	0205 4.5	0725 0.9	1446 4.6	1948 1.3
7	Tu	0247 4.3	0810 1.1	1532 4.5	2038 1.5
8	W	0336 4.2	0901 1.3	1621 4.3	2131 1.7
9	Th	0430 4.0	0958 1.5	1717 4.2	2234 1.8
10	F	0534 3.8	1103 1.7	1827 4.0	2342 1.8
11	Sa	0645 3.7	1212 1.8	1919 4.0	
12	Su	0048 1.7	0754 3.8	1315 1.7	2017 4.0
13	M	0146 1.6	0853 3.9	1409 1.6	2108 4.1
14	Tu	0235 1.5	0942 4.1	1501 1.5	2154 4.3
15	W	0317 1.3	1025 4.2	1534 1.3	2234 4.4
16	Th	0355 1.2	1102 4.3	1611 1.2	2310 4.4
17 ○	F	0430 1.0	1137 4.3	1647 1.1	2345 4.4
18	Sa	0506 0.9	1212 4.4	1726 1.0	
19	Su	0021 4.4	0543 0.8	1251 4.4	1804 1.0
20	M	0059 4.4	0622 0.7	1334 4.5	1845 1.0
21	Tu	0140 4.4	0703 0.7	1420 4.5	1925 1.0
22	W	0224 4.4	0745 0.7	1506 4.5	2009 1.0
23	Th	0311 4.3	0831 0.8	1554 4.4	2055 1.1
24	F	0402 4.2	0910 1.0	1646 4.3	2151 1.3
25	Sa	0459 4.1	1024 1.1	1742 4.2	2259 1.4
26	Su	0612 4.0	1134 1.3	1853 4.2	
27	M	0015 1.4	0728 4.0	1252 1.5	2001 4.3
28	Tu	0130 1.3	0840 4.2	1402 1.3	2105 4.4
29	W	0234 1.1	0942 4.3	1501 1.1	2203 4.5
30	Th	0331 0.9	1039 4.5	1554 0.9	2256 4.6
31 ●	F	0421 0.7	1130 4.6	1642 0.9	2344 4.8

AUGUST

Day		Tide 1	Tide 2	Tide 3	Tide 4
1	Sa	0506 0.7	1216 4.6	1725 0.9	
2	Su	0026 4.6	0547 0.7	1259 4.7	1807 0.9
3	M	0107 4.5	0626 0.8	1340 4.7	1846 1.0
4	Tu	0145 4.5	0703 0.8	1419 4.6	1925 1.2
5	W	0223 4.4	0742 1.0	1459 4.6	2005 1.3
6	Th	0304 4.2	0824 1.2	1539 4.4	2048 1.5
7	F	0348 4.1	0910 1.4	1622 4.2	2138 1.7
8	Sa	0440 3.9	1006 1.6	1715 4.0	2240 1.9
9	Su	0544 3.7	1113 1.9	1819 3.8	2353 1.9
10	M	0701 3.6	1228 2.0	1929 3.8	
11	Tu	0105 1.9	0815 3.7	1336 1.9	2033 3.9
12	W	0206 1.7	0914 3.9	1430 1.7	2127 4.1
13	Th	0254 1.4	1001 4.1	1514 1.4	2212 4.2
14	F	0333 1.2	1039 4.3	1552 1.2	2250 4.4
15 ○	Sa	0411 1.0	1115 4.5	1630 1.0	2325 4.5
16	Su	0447 0.8	1151 4.5	1709 0.9	
17	M	0002 4.5	0527 0.7	1231 4.6	1749 0.8
18	Tu	0041 4.6	0608 0.7	1315 4.7	1830 0.8
19	W	0124 4.6	0651 0.5	1401 4.7	1912 0.7
20	Th	0209 4.6	0733 0.5	1447 4.7	1953 0.8
21	F	0256 4.5	0817 0.7	1533 4.6	2038 1.0
22	Sa	0346 4.3	0904 1.0	1623 4.4	2131 1.3
23	Su	0444 4.1	1004 1.3	1723 4.2	2240 1.5
24	M	0558 3.9	1121 1.6	1836 4.0	
25	Tu	0004 1.6	0724 3.9	1246 1.7	1954 4.1
26	W	0125 1.5	0841 4.1	1359 1.5	2102 4.2
27	Th	0232 1.2	0941 4.3	1459 1.3	2158 4.3
28	F	0326 1.0	1033 4.5	1548 1.1	2246 4.5
29	Sa	0411 0.8	1117 4.6	1631 0.9	2329 4.6
30	Su	0451 0.7	1157 4.7	1711 0.7	
31	M	0008 4.6	0530 0.7	1236 4.7	1749 0.9

Fig. 23 Tidal heights, Portsmouth.

The tide tables give the times of high and low water in GMT, now quoted as universal time (UT) or co-ordinated universal time (UTC).

Notice that at the top of the page in Fig. 23 a reference is made to zone time UT (GMT), and a warning given regarding the UK's change to BST (British summer time): one hour is added to GMT to produce BST on 21 March, and it is removed on 22 Oct.

GMT and Zone Times

The solar day controls our daily lives, and all our activities are timed by the passage of the sun across our sky. Noon – that is, 1200 local mean time (LMT) – occurs when the sun is crossing the observer's meridian: it is at its highest point in the sky and said to be 'at its culmination'.

Although we all know that the earth orbits the sun, to the earthly observer the sun moves across our sky from east to west, completing one 360° revolution every twenty-four hours. That is the period of the solar day, completed at a mean rotational speed of 15°/hour. If we could stand off in space we would notice that when local noon occurs at Greenwich, the LMT at a position 90° east of Greenwich is 1800 of that same day, ie noon at this second position occurred six hours earlier, because the sun appeared to cross that position's meridian on its apparent westward passage. At this same instant the LMT at a position 90° west of Greenwich would be 0600 of that same day, and local noon here would occur some six hours later when the sun would be overhead. These details are shown on Fig. 24, together with the 'International Date Line' (IDT). This position 180° E/W

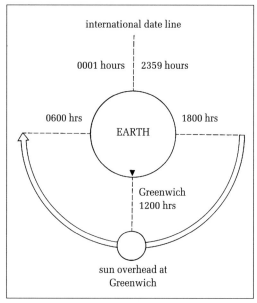

Fig. 24 Local mean time.

of Greenwich is a necessary feature resulting from LMT. Immediately to the left of this line on our day in question, the LMT would be 0001; immediately to its right the LMT would be 2359 of that same day.

The International Date Line

At the instant of local noon at Greenwich, the LMT at the position immediately east of the IDL is 0001 hours of the same day, whereas at the position immediately west of the IDL the LMT is 2359 of that same day. Imagine now a vessel about to cross the IDL in a westerly direction at 0001 on a Monday morning: as it crosses the IDL, the LMT would become 0001 on Wednesday – the intervening Tuesday would simply not exist to that crossing vessel. And a vessel about to cross the IDL in an easterly direction at 2359 LMT on Monday would have two Mondays that week because as she crossed the IDL her LMT would revert to 0001 of that same Monday.

Local mean time, a very human and necessary facility, produces a requirement for an internationally recognized time reference. Tide tables for example are printed with reference to LMT. In the UK almanac, ports on the French coast have their tidal heights listed against local mean time, and differ by one hour from UK mean time. This is not a great difference, and a yacht on passage from Portsmouth to St Malo need not be too concerned by it; however, if the French destination was a 'locked' port, the 'time-careless' navigator may have to anchor off until the port 'opens' again.

The LMT is maintained on all sea-going vessels, together with the LMT at Greenwich. Greenwich is the internationally recognized time reference, until recently called Greenwich mean time (GMT), but now often referred to as universal time (UT). In order to relate LMT to GMT the world is divided into twenty-four time zones, each one occupying 15° of longitude. Time zone 0 is centred on the Greenwich meridian covering the area 7.5°E to 7.5°W of Greenwich. The zones east of Greenwich are numbered one through to twelve with a negative prefix: −1 to −12. The zones west of Greenwich are numbered +1 to +12, though conventionally the + prefix is not normally shown on documentation. Time zone 12 straddles the IDL and is consequently two 'half' time zones, each covering 7.5° of longitude and signed −12 and +12. The time-zoned earth is shown at Fig. 25.

Using the time-zoned data, local time anywhere on the earth is now easily converted to the international time reference by making an algebraic sum of local mean

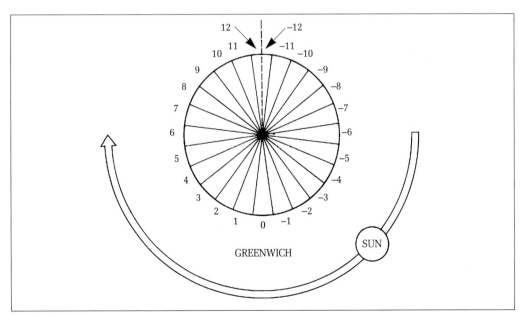

Fig. 25 Time zones.

TIME ZONE -0100
(French Standard Time)
Subtract 1 hour for GMT
For French Summer Time add
ONE hour in non-shaded area

FRANCE, NORTH COAST — DIEPPE

Lat 49°56' N   Long   1°05' E

TIMES AND HEIGHTS OF HIGH AND LOW WATERS

MAY

Day	Time	m	Time	m	Time	m	Time	m
1 F	0342	1.5	0921	8.3	1612	1.2	2148	8.5
2 Sa	0439	1.0	1013	8.9	1705	1.2	2237	9.0
3 Su ●	0530	0.6	1100	9.3	1754	0.4	2323	9.4
4 M	0618	0.3	1146	9.6	1841	0.3		
5 Tu	0008	9.6	0703	0.3	1231	9.7	1925	0.3
6 W	0054	9.7	0746	0.3	1316	9.6	2009	0.4
7 Th	0138	9.5	0831	0.5	1402	9.3	2052	0.7
8 F	0223	9.1	0912	0.8	1445	8.8	2134	1.1
9 Sa	0308	8.6	0956	1.3	1532	8.1	2220	1.6
10 Su	0358	8.0	1047	1.8	1628	7.6	2317	2.1
11 M	0500	7.5	1151	2.2	1737	7.0		
12 Tu	0029	2.5	0618	7.3	1309	2.4	1900	7.0
13 W	0152	2.4	0741	7.4	1432	2.2	2016	7.2
14 Th	0307	2.0	0848	7.6	1539	1.8	2116	7.6
15 F	0406	1.8	0942	8.0	1632	1.6	2205	8.0
16 Sa	0455	1.6	1026	8.3	1718	1.4	2245	8.3
17 Su	0636	1.3	1103	8.6	1754	1.2	2321	8.5
18 M ○	0612	1.1	1137	8.6	1830	1.1	2354	8.7
19 Tu	0648	1.1	1210	8.7	1902	1.1		
20 W	0027	8.8	0718	1.0	1243	8.7	1934	1.1
21 Th	0100	8.7	0749	1.1	1316	8.6	2005	1.2
22 F	0132	8.6	0821	1.1	1348	8.4	2037	1.4
23 Sa	0206	8.3	0852	1.4	1422	8.1	2109	1.6
24 Su	0240	8.2	0926	1.6	1459	7.8	2145	1.9
25 M	0319	7.9	1006	1.9	1541	7.6	2229	2.1
26 Tu	0407	7.6	1054	2.2	1634	7.2	2323	2.3
27 W	0507	7.4	1156	2.2	1743	7.1		
28 Th	0033	2.3	0622	7.5	1312	2.0	1901	7.4
29 F	0151	2.0	0737	8.0	1427	1.7	2012	7.9
30 Sa	0302	1.5	0843	8.3	1533	1.2	2112	8.5
31 Su	0403	1.1	0941	8.8	1632	0.9	2207	8.9

JUNE

Day	Time	m	Time	m	Time	m	Time	m
1 M	0459	0.7	1033	9.2	1727	0.6	2258	9.3
2 Tu ●	0553	0.5	1123	9.4	1819	0.5	2348	9.5
3 W	0643	0.4	1211	9.4	1907	0.5		
4 Th	0036	9.6	0731	0.4	1301	9.3	1954	0.6
5 F	0125	9.4	0817	0.6	1348	9.1	2040	0.8
6 Sa	0211	9.1	0901	0.9	1434	8.7	2122	1.2
7 Su	0256	8.7	0944	1.2	1519	8.2	2206	1.5
8 M	0343	8.2	1031	1.6	1608	7.7	2256	2.0
9 Tu	0435	7.8	1123	2.0	1706	7.3	2354	2.3
10 W	0537	7.5	1226	2.2	1812	7.1		
11 Th	0101	2.4	0648	7.3	1337	2.3	1924	7.1
12 F	0212	2.3	0757	7.4	1445	2.1	2027	7.4
13 Sa	0316	2.1	0855	7.6	1544	2.0	2121	7.7
14 Su	0411	1.9	0945	7.8	1635	1.7	2208	8.0
15 M	0458	1.6	1029	8.1	1719	1.6	2249	8.3
16 Tu	0540	1.4	1107	8.3	1759	1.4	2326	8.5
17 W ○	0619	1.3	1145	8.4	1838	1.3		
18 Th	0003	8.6	0655	1.2	1221	8.5	1913	1.2
19 F	0038	8.7	0730	1.1	1257	8.5	1947	1.2
20 Sa	0115	8.7	0805	1.1	1333	8.5	2022	1.3
21 Su	0151	8.6	0841	1.2	1409	8.3	2057	1.4
22 M	0228	8.5	0915	1.3	1447	8.1	2134	1.5
23 Tu	0307	8.3	0953	1.5	1528	7.9	2215	1.7
24 W	0351	8.1	1038	1.6	1617	7.7	2303	1.8
25 Th	0443	7.9	1132	1.8	1714	7.6		
26 F	0002	1.9	0547	7.8	1236	1.8	1822	7.7
27 Sa	0111	1.8	0658	8.0	1348	1.6	1934	7.9
28 Su	0224	1.6	0808	8.2	1459	1.4	2041	8.3
29 M	0332	1.3	0912	8.6	1605	1.1	2143	8.7
30 Tu	0436	1.0	1012	8.8	1706	0.9	2240	9.0

JULY

Day	Time	m	Time	M	Time	M	Time	M
1 W ●	0536	0.8	1107	9.0	1804	0.8	2333	9.2
2 Th	0631	0.6	1159	9.1	1856	0.7		
3 F	0025	9.3	0720	0.6	1250	9.1	1944	0.7
4 Sa	0114	9.3	0806	0.7	1336	9.0	2028	0.8
5 Su	0159	9.1	0848	0.8	1420	8.7	2108	1.1
6 M	0240	8.8	0927	1.1	1501	8.4	2147	1.4
7 Tu	0321	8.5	1007	1.4	1542	8.0	2228	1.7
8 W	0404	8.1	1050	1.7	1627	7.6	2312	2.0
9 Th	0451	7.7	1137	2.1	1718	7.2		
10 F	0005	2.3	0547	7.3	1235	2.3	1820	7.0
11 Sa	0107	2.5	0654	7.2	1343	2.5	1928	7.0
12 Su	0217	2.5	0801	7.2	1450	2.4	2032	7.2
13 M	0322	2.3	0902	7.4	1552	2.2	2129	7.6
14 Tu	0420	2.0	0954	7.6	1645	1.9	2218	7.9
15 W	0509	1.7	1040	7.9	1732	1.6	2301	8.3
16 Th ○	0654	1.4	1122	8.2	1816	1.4	2341	8.5
17 F	0636	1.2	1201	8.5	1854	1.2		
18 Sa	0021	8.8	0713	1.1	1239	8.6	1932	1.1
19 Su	0059	8.9	0749	1.0	1318	8.7	2008	1.0
20 M	0136	8.9	0827	0.9	1356	8.7	2045	1.0
21 Tu	0215	8.9	0902	1.0	1434	8.6	2120	1.1
22 W	0252	8.6	0939	1.1	1513	8.4	2159	1.3
23 Th	0333	8.6	1020	1.2	1556	8.2	2242	1.4
24 F	0419	8.3	1106	1.5	1646	8.0	2334	1.6
25 Sa	0516	8.1	1203	1.8	1747	7.8		
26 Su	0037	1.8	0624	7.9	1314	1.8	1901	7.8
27 M	0152	1.7	0741	7.9	1433	1.7	2018	8.0
28 Tu	0311	1.5	1002	8.5	1548	1.5	2129	8.4
29 W	0423	1.3	1002	8.5	1656	1.2	2231	8.7
30 Th	0527	1.1	1059	9.2	1755	1.0	2326	9.0
31 F ●	0622	0.8	1151	8.8	1847	0.8		

AUGUST

Day	Time	M	Time	M	Time	M	Time	M
1 Sa	0016	9.2	0710	0.7	1238	9.0	1932	0.8
2 Su	0101	9.3	0752	0.6	1322	9.0	2013	0.8
3 M	0141	9.2	0832	0.7	1401	8.9	2049	0.9
4 Tu	0218	9.0	0906	0.9	1436	8.6	2121	1.2
5 W	0253	8.7	0939	1.2	1511	8.3	2155	1.5
6 Th	0328	8.3	1013	1.5	1547	7.8	2231	1.8
7 F	0406	7.8	1050	2.0	1627	7.4	2311	2.2
8 Sa	0450	7.3	1135	2.4	1716	7.0		
9 Su	0003	2.6	0546	6.9	1235	2.7	1821	6.8
10 M	0111	2.8	0659	6.8	1350	2.8	1937	6.8
11 Tu	0230	2.7	0815	6.9	1507	2.6	2050	7.2
12 W	0342	2.3	0921	7.3	1613	2.2	2149	7.6
13 Th	0441	1.9	1015	7.7	1707	1.6	2238	8.1
14 F ○	0531	1.5	1100	8.2	1753	1.4	2321	8.7
15 Sa	0615	1.2	1141	8.6	1835	1.1		
16 Su	0001	8.9	0654	0.9	1221	8.8	1913	0.9
17 M	0040	9.2	0732	0.7	1300	9.0	1950	0.7
18 Tu	0119	9.3	0809	0.6	1337	9.1	2028	0.7
19 W	0157	9.3	0846	0.6	1415	9.0	2103	0.7
20 Th	0234	9.2	0920	0.7	1453	8.9	2140	0.9
21 F	0313	8.9	1000	1.0	1533	8.6	2220	1.2
22 Sa	0356	8.5	1043	1.4	1620	8.2	2307	1.6
23 Su	0448	8.0	1136	1.8	1720	7.8		
24 M	0010	1.9	0557	7.6	1249	2.1	1839	7.5
25 Tu	0133	2.1	0724	7.5	1418	2.1	2007	7.7
26 W	0302	1.8	0848	7.8	1542	1.8	2125	8.1
27 Th	0418	1.5	0957	8.2	1652	1.4	2227	8.6
28 F ●	0621	1.1	1054	8.6	1747	1.1	2318	9.0
29 Sa	0612	0.9	1140	8.9	1835	0.9		
30 Su	0002	9.2	0656	0.7	1223	9.0	1915	0.7
31 M	0041	9.3	0733	0.6	1301	9.1	1950	0.7

Fig. 26 Tide tables, Dieppe.

time and zone time. For example, a location 090° east is in time zone –6, and from our example above its local time of 1800 is the equivalent of 1200 UT, noon at Greenwich: that is:

$$1800(LMT)–6(time\ zone)=1200(UT)$$

The European yachtsman travelling between UK (TZ = 0000) and continental ports (TZ = –0100) will obtain tidal information from the relevant pages of the almanac. The time data on these pages is given in LMT, so the data for French ports (TZ=–0100) would need to be converted to UK times (TZ=0000) when passage planning. For example, using Fig. 26, the tidal table for Dieppe (TZ=–0100): the LMT of LW at Dieppe on the morning of Monday 11 May is 1151; the TZ of –0100 gives the GMT of the HW at Dieppe of 1151–0100 = 1051 GMT.

The Twelfths Rule

This rule assumes a sinusoidal shape to the rise and fall of the tide, and a twelve-hour period from low water through high water and back to the next low water. It further assumes that the rise in sea level follows this sequence:

During the first and the sixth hour after LW: rises by one-twelfth of the range;
During the second and the fifth hour after LW: rises by two-twelfths of the range;
During the third and the fourth hour after LW: rises by three-twelfths of the range.

The final assumption is that the fall of tide from HW to LW follows the same hourly pattern as the rise. Fig. 27 illustrates the twelfths rule.

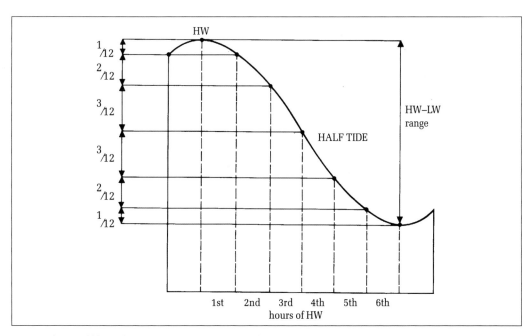

Fig 27 The Twelfths Rule. Assumptions are sinusoidal tide of 12 hours duration HW to HW.

For example, assuming a tidal range of 4.6m, calculate the rise of tide 2½ hours after LW using the twelfths rule:

Rise during the first hour
$$= \frac{1}{12} \times 4.6 = 0.38\text{m}$$
Rise during the second hour
$$= \frac{2}{12} \times 4.6 = 0.76\text{m}$$
Rise during the last half hour
$$= \frac{1}{2} \times \frac{3}{12} \times 4.6 = 0.55\text{m}$$

Total rise in 2½ hours = 1.69m

Examination of an actual port's tidal curve will usually show only a passing resemblance to the fabricated twelfths curve: in other words, the shape and timing of the twelfths rule tide can bear little relationship to the actual tide you may be experiencing. Nonetheless it can be a useful check on your tidal predictions. Tidal calculations are completed using the correct tide curve and data for your port of interest, see below; then the twelfths rule should produce a reasonable comparison.

Tidal Curves

The twelfths rule assumes a sinusoidal rise and fall of tide, but in fact a quick skim through the tidal curves of individual ports given in a nautical almanac will show that this is only an approximation. Fig. 28 is a copy of the tidal curve and tide table for Portsmouth: the curve shows the predicted characteristic curve for the full tidal period of LW through HW and back to LW, and is most certainly far from sinusoidal. Notice also from Fig. 28 how the curve for a neap tide, the dotted rise and fall, differs from the full line of the spring tide. The boxes along the base line of the curve allow the navigator to enter the time

of HW and the hourly intervals before and after this time. The problem with using these boxes is that most ports do not experience a 'twelfths rule' tide, nor even tides where LW is 'exactly' five, six or seven hours either side of HW. The curve for Portsmouth is so far off being symmetrical that the time of flood tide differs considerably from the time of ebb, the curve showing a seven-hour flood period and five hours of ebb. The Portsmouth tide table for 11 May from Fig. 23 gives a flood tide from 1012 to 1742, ie flooding for seven hours and thirty minutes; but this time will not fit the time boxes for the seven hours before HW – there is a half-hour discrepancy. The answer to this problem is, when working near the time of LW, fill the boxes from the LW end.

Figs 29 and 30 are copies of Dover's tidal curve and tide table, and this port's tidal curve is also far from the idealized curve of the twelfths' rule.

The navigator wishing to enter a particular port obtains from the nautical tide tables, the time and height of low water for the date in question, and the LAT from the appropriate chart. He then calculates the depth of water, and compares this depth with the yacht's draught, to determine whether entry or departure can be made at any state of the tide. In situations where the depth at low water is too low, the mariner must wait for a 'rise of tide' which will satisfy the following:

Rise of tide + LW + LAT >= yacht's draught

For example, for a yacht drawing 2.2m:

LW = 0.7m
LAT = 0.2m
draught = 2.2m

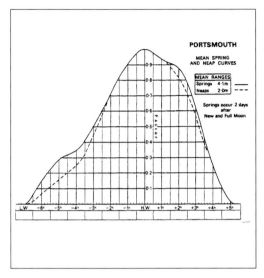

Fig. 28 Portsmouth, tidal curve.

At low water the depth would be 0.9m, so entry would be delayed until the tide had risen at least 1.3m above its low water level. This is the absolute minimum depth required, and in a perfectly flat calm and over a soft bottom it may just be adequate; however, it would be far better to add a little, say 0.5m, for safety – that is, a rise of 1.8m. The tidal curve for the port in question allows the mariner to calculate the earliest time, after LW, that the depth of water will allow him to float.

The tidal curve for Dover, Fig. 29, has two parts: part (i) is a graph, and you may wish to turn the diagram through 90° to see the graph in its proper perspective. The left-hand scale (a) of Fig. 29(i) allows the height of HW to be entered; the right-

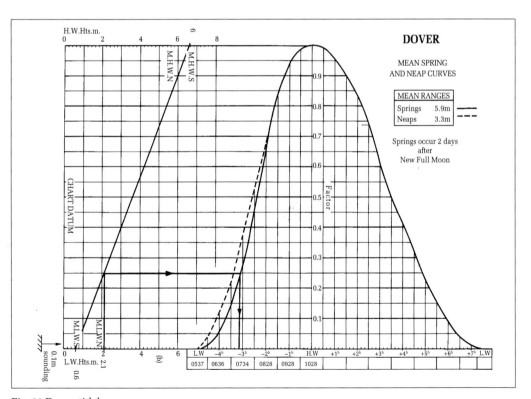

Fig. 29 Dover, tidal curve.

TIME ZONE UT (GMT)
Summer Time add ONE hour in non-shaded area

ENGLAND, SOUTH COAST — DOVER

Lat 51°07′ N Long 1°19′ E

TIMES AND HEIGHTS OF HIGH AND LOW WATERS

	MAY				JUNE				JULY				AUGUST		
	Time	m		Time	m		Time	m		Time	m		Time	m		Time	m		Time	m		Time	m		Time	m

	Time	m	Time	m		Time	m	Time	m		Time	m	Time	m		Time	m	Time	m
1 F	0327 0826 1553 2049	1·2 6·0 1·2 6·3	**16** Sa	0447 0939 1706 2149	1·2 6·9 1·2 6·2	**1** M	0444 0938 1706 2159	0·8 6·5 0·9 6·7	**16** Tu	0618 1024 1734 2237	1·3 6·1 1·3 6·2	**1** W	0520 1020 1742 2238	0·9 6·5 1·0 6·6	**16** Th	0630 1037 1754 2247	1·2 6·2 1·2 6·2	**1** Sa	0713 1144 1927	0·9 6·7 0·8	**16** Su	0638 1118 1902 2332	1·0 6·8 0·9 6·5
2 Sa	0424 0912 1647 2135	0·8 6·4 0·9 6·6	**17** Su	0625 1013 1740 2226	1·1 6·1 1·2 6·3	**2** Tu	0537 1028 1757 2248	0·6 6·6 0·7 6·8	**17** W	0654 1101 1814 2312	1·1 6·3 1·1 6·3	**2** Th	0621 1112 1839 2330	0·8 6·6 0·8 6·6	**17** F	0614 1109 1836 2319	1·1 6·3 1·1 6·3	**2** Su	0004 0759 1224 2011	6·6 0·9 6·7 0·7	**17** M	0717 1156 1938	0·9 6·7 0·8
3 Su	0516 0957 1736 2220	0·6 6·8 0·7 6·8	**18** M	0556 1048 1807 2302	1·1 6·2 1·1 6·4	**3** W	0629 1120 1848 2339	0·6 6·7 0·7 6·8	**18** Th	0634 1133 1853 2343	1·0 6·3 1·0 6·2	**3** F	0716 1200 1933	0·8 6·7 0·7	**18** Sa	0655 1143 1917 2354	1·0 6·4 1·0 6·3	**3** M	0043 0837 1302 2050	6·5 0·9 6·7 0·8	**18** Tu	0011 0749 1235 2009	6·6 0·9 6·8 0·8
4 M	0604 1044 1821 2306	0·5 6·8 0·6 6·9	**19** Tu	0624 1122 1838 2336	1·0 6·3 1·0 6·4	**4** Th	0721 1205 1938	0·6 6·7 0·6	**19** F	0712 1206 1931	1·0 6·3 1·0	**4** Sa	0019 0806 1243 2022	6·6 0·9 6·6 0·7	**19** Su	0733 1218 1954	1·0 6·5 0·9	**4** Tu	0123 0910 1340 2124	6·4 1·1 6·6 1·0	**19** W	0055 0819 1317 2042	6·6 0·9 6·7 0·8
5 Tu	0649 1133 1904 2354	0·4 6·8 0·5 6·9	**20** W	0656 1154 1912	0·9 6·3 1·0	**5** F	0031 0811 1300 2027	6·7 0·6 6·6 0·7	**20** Sa	0014 0748 1238 2006	6·2 1·0 6·3 1·1	**5** Su	0104 0851 1326 2107	6·5 0·9 6·5 0·8	**20** M	0032 0806 1257 2027	6·4 1·0 6·5 0·9	**5** W	0201 0936 1419 2155	6·2 1·4 6·4 1·3	**20** Th	0138 0854 1359 2119	6·5 1·1 6·6 0·9
6 W	0733 1224 1949	0·4 6·8 0·5	**21** Th	0005 0730 1224 1947	6·3 0·9 6·3 1·0	**6** Sa	0120 0900 1345 2118	6·5 0·9 6·4 0·8	**21** Su	0048 0822 1313 2042	6·2 1·1 6·3 1·1	**6** M	0147 0934 1406 2150	6·3 1·1 6·4 1·0	**21** Tu	0114 0850 1338 2101	6·4 1·1 6·4 1·0	**6** Th	0243 1000 1501 2226	6·0 1·6 6·2 1·5	**21** F	0226 0934 1446 2200	6·3 1·1 6·3 1·1
7 Th	0043 0818 1314 2034	6·8 0·5 6·6 0·6	**22** F	0031 0804 1252 2022	6·2 0·9 6·2 1·1	**7** Su	0208 0948 1430 2207	6·2 1·1 6·2 1·1	**22** M	0126 0858 1352 2118	6·1 1·2 6·2 1·2	**7** Tu	0232 1012 1461 2231	6·1 1·4 6·2 1·3	**22** W	0159 0915 1420 2141	6·3 1·1 6·3 1·1	**7** F	0328 1031 1549 2302	5·7 1·9 5·9 1·8	**22** Sa	0317 1020 1538 2251	6·1 1·4 6·1 1·4
8 F	0133 0904 1402 2124	6·5 0·7 6·4 0·8	**23** Sa	0057 0839 1323 2056	6·1 1·1 6·1 1·3	**8** M	0257 1037 1519 2269	5·9 1·4 6·0 1·4	**23** Tu	0211 0936 1437 2159	6·0 1·3 6·1 1·3	**8** W	0319 1049 1541 2313	5·8 1·7 6·0 1·6	**23** Th	0249 0956 1510 2224	6·1 1·3 6·2 1·4	**8** Sa	0421 1112 1645 2349	5·4 2·1 5·6 2·1	**23** Su	0416 1115 1641 2357	5·8 1·7 5·8 1·7
9 Sa	0223 0956 1450 2216	6·2 1·1 6·1 1·2	**24** Su	0131 0912 1359 2134	5·9 1·3 5·9 1·4	**9** Tu	0353 1129 1617 2356	5·7 1·7 5·8 1·6	**24** W	0304 1019 1532 2247	5·8 1·5 5·9 1·4	**9** Th	0414 1129 1637	5·6 1·9 5·8	**24** F	0343 1044 1604 2316	6·0 1·5 6·0 1·4	**9** Su	0529 1205 1757	5·2 2·4 5·3	**24** M	0525 1229 1756	5·6 1·9 5·6
10 Su	0318 1051 1545 2318	5·9 1·6 5·8 1·5	**25** M	0215 0952 1449 2216	5·7 1·6 5·8 1·6	**10** W	0459 1227 1723	6·4 1·9 5·6	**25** Th	0409 1111 1634 2346	5·7 1·6 5·9 1·5	**10** F	0000 1214 1742	1·8 2·2 5·6	**25** Sa	0444 1142 1708	5·8 1·7 5·9	**10** M	0046 1313 1917	2·2 2·4 5·2	**25** Tu	0120 1357 1923	1·9 1·9 5·6
11 M	0421 1157 1651	5·5 1·7 5·5	**26** Tu	0314 1040 1550 2309	5·5 1·7 5·6 1·7	**11** Th	0069 0617 1328 1836	1·7 5·4 1·8 5·6	**26** F	0516 1214 1742	1·7 1·7 5·9	**11** Sa	0052 0631 1310 1863	2·0 5·3 2·1 5·5	**26** Su	0021 0551 1252 1818	1·6 6·7 1·8 5·8	**11** Tu	0158 0801 1421 2020	2·2 5·3 2·3 5·4	**26** W	0249 0816 1521 2047	1·7 5·7 1·6 5·8
12 Tu	0027 0544 1309 1812	1·6 5·3 1·9 5·4	**27** W	0430 1139 1705	5·4 1·7 5·6	**12** F	0206 0724 1436 1940	1·8 5·4 2·0 5·7	**27** Sa	0056 0624 1326 1848	1·5 1·6 1·6 6·0	**12** Su	0157 0738 1420 1957	2·1 5·4 2·2 5·6	**27** M	0137 0703 1411 1930	1·6 6·0 1·7 5·8	**12** W	0317 0853 1550 2110	2·0 5·8 1·9 5·8	**27** Th	0406 0922 1633 2148	1·5 6·0 1·3 6·1
13 W	0142 0713 1423 1928	1·6 6·4 1·8 5·6	**28** Th	0017 0550 1250 1819	1·7 5·5 1·8 5·7	**13** Sa	0311 0819 1535 2033	1·6 5·6 1·8 6·9	**28** Su	0208 0727 1437 1949	1·3 5·9 1·6 6·1	**13** M	0304 0834 1527 2050	1·9 5·8 2·0 5·7	**28** Tu	0256 0815 1527 2039	1·6 5·9 1·1 6·0	**13** Th	0416 0934 1644 2148	1·7 5·8 1·5 6·9	**28** F	0515 1009 1734 2233	1·2 6·3 1·0 6·4
14 Th	0256 0816 1529 2025	1·5 5·8 1·6 5·8	**29** F	0135 0657 1406 1923	1·5 5·7 1·6 6·0	**14** Su	0402 0905 1620 2118	1·6 5·8 1·7 6·0	**29** M	0317 0826 1542 2049	1·2 6·1 1·3 6·3	**14** Tu	0369 0921 1823 2135	1·7 6·1 1·7 5·9	**29** W	0409 0922 1634 2142	1·3 6·1 1·3 6·2	**14** F	0506 1009 1733 2220	1·3 6·2 1·1 6·1	**29** Sa	0614 1048 1829 2309	1·0 6·6 0·9 6·5
15 F	0357 0901 1624 2110	1·3 6·8 1·4 6·0	**30** Sa	0247 0755 1512 2018	1·2 6·0 1·3 6·3	**15** M	0442 0946 1658 2200	1·4 6·0 1·5 6·2	**30** Tu	0420 0924 1644 2143	1·2 6·3 1·1 6·5	**15** W	0445 1002 1709 2214	1·5 6·0 1·4 6·0	**30** Th	0516 1017 1737 2235	1·1 6·4 1·1 6·4	**15** Sa	0544 1042 1818 2264	1·1 6·6 1·0 6·4	**30** Su	0702 1125 1914 2344	0·9 6·7 0·8 6·5
			31 Su	0349 0847 1612 2108	1·0 6·3 1·1 6·5							**31** F	0619 1102 1835 2322	1·0 6·3 0·9 6·5				**31** M	0741 1201 1952	0·9 6·8 0·8

Fig. 30 Dover, tide table.

hand scale (b) is for the height of LW to be entered. Since HW and LW are measured above LAT, this means that the baseline of this graph is at LAT, therefore soundings will be below the baseline and drying heights will be above it. As an example, values for the morning tide at Dover on 2 June, obtained from Fig. 30 – LW @ 0537 (0.6m) and HW @ 1028 (6.6m) – have been entered on Fig. 29(i), and are shown joined by a fine straight line. Turn the diagram back through 90° and note part (ii): this is the tidal curve. At the bottom of the curve are the baseline time boxes. Enter the time of HW (1028 (GMT)) in the centre box, and in the boxes for the period of rise (–1,–2,–3 etc) enter the hourly intervals before HW, ie 0928, 0828 and 0728.

Now let us assume that a yacht drawing 2.2m is to enter Dover on a neap tide and berth in a location where the LAT is only 0.1m. The minimum height of tide required is 2.1m (draught-LAT), but since the height of tide at LW is only 0.6m, clearly the yacht cannot berth at LW. In our graph the height of tide required has been entered – 2.1m at (c) of Fig. 28 – extended to meet our line joining HW/LW, then projected to cut the tidal curve on a rising spring tide; the line is then dropped to meet the baseline time boxes. The centre of the time box is three hours and twenty minutes before HW, in this case 0728 GMT, and interpolation within the box gives the earliest time to enter as 0724 GMT.

In the above example we started by deducing the depth required, entered the scale with this value, and by reference to the curve obtained the time at which the required minimum depth would be reached. The prudent mariner will also allow for:

(i) sea chop and wave height;
(ii) the date LAT was recorded;
(iii) high pressure weather;
(iv) the fact that our calculations are only predictions.

All the above factors could – and just to make things awkward, usually *would* – give less depth than calculated. In this example we have entered on a rising tide and so touching a soft bottom may be only a momentary embarrassment; however, if entering or leaving on a falling tide it is good practice to add one metre or more, depending on the conditions prevailing, to the minimum depth required.

On some occasions we would use the above tide graph and curve in the reverse order to the above – for example when planning an arrival time, that is, in deciding to make for a particular port during a cruise: let the port be Dover with the tidal details as used in Fig. 29. The skipper would calculate the estimated time of arrival and compare it with the time of HW at the port in question. Let us assume that his yacht draws 1.7m and desires a safety margin of 0.5m – that is, a required minimum depth of 2.2m on arrival; it is 10 n. m. off the port, making 5 knots, with the port dead ahead. The ETA is therefore two hours away. A reference to the port's tidal curve will allow comparison of the ETA time with the time of HW. Assuming that the yacht will arrive four hours before HW, in this case 0636 GMT, enter the appropriate time box at the base of the curve, extend the entry point to cut the tidal curve, project this point on the curve down to the line on the graph, joining HW to LW, and hence read the height of tide at our ETA. From Fig. 30 the height of tide at 0636 is only 1.3m. With this information the skipper then checks the chart for LAT values.

The above use of the curve and graph provides useful tide information some two hours before arrival and permits the skipper to plan in detail how his entry will be made.

The importance of a mariner's ability to use tide tables, graphs and curves correctly cannot be overstated; going aground on an unknown seabed is never funny, yet the only reason for many yachts grounding has been a miscalculation or a lazy reliance on the twelfths rule. If the bottom is soft the yacht may well float clear on the next flood; but consider what may happen if the waters are falling ... moving the crew around the boat, reversing the engine and sitting out on the boom may all be to no avail, in which case the yacht, assuming she is single keel, will slowly but definitely heel over, and eventually lie on her side on drying ground. Immediate concerns which would undoubtedly spring to mind include: is this ebbing tide the highest spring of the year? What will she lie on? Sharp piercing rock, an uneven rock-strewn seabed, an old broken anchor fluke? And if she is damaged as she settles, will she fill with water on the next flood?

Depth of Water to Anchor in

When intending to anchor overnight with a falling tide, a skipper needs but two pieces of information:

1) the yacht's draught plus a safety margin;
2) how much the water is going to fall between the time of anchoring and LW.

If he doesn't know the first, then he shouldn't be skipper. The second piece of information is read from the tide table and curves for the area he intends to anchor in. The base time boxes of the curve are entered with the intended time of anchoring, a line is drawn to cut the curve, and extended to cut his HW-LW line; from this can be read the value of height of tide at that time. The value of low water is subtracted from this value to obtain the height of tide, which is in fact the amount by which the water will fall between the time of anchoring and LW. Adding together the draught (say, 1.8m), a safety figure (say, 0.5m) and the height of tide obtained as above (say, 1.6m) gives a required depth of water of 3.9m. With this information the skipper approaches the shoreline of a gently shoaling bay, observing the echo sounder until it shows 3.9m under the keel, at which point the anchor can be 'let go' with the appropriate amount of anchor line.

The crew will sleep soundly knowing that at LW there will be 0.5m under the keel. During the night as the tide turns the yacht will swing round on her anchor, and inevitably – because that is the way of such things – she will swing round shorewards, ie over shallower water; but of course the prudent skipper will have allowed for this in the safety margin...

Secondary Ports

Secondary ports are generally smaller and have less commercial traffic than a standard port. Every secondary port is related to a nearby standard port, and is assumed to have the same characteristic tidal curve; however, the times and heights of high and low waters usually differ, and it

French port at high water: but when it dries...

The same port at low water – it really dries!

is these differences which are published in the tide almanacs. Fig. 31 is a copy of the tide predictions for the secondary port of Margate, and to remind you, Fig. 30 is the tide table for the associated standard port, Dover; in the almanac, the arrow indicates the direction in which to go in order to find the standard port's tidal data. The following details are given in Fig. 31:

Margate is in Kent.
The important charts are listed.
Mean water times are 0000 difference on Dover.
Mean level of water is 3.7m.
Mean duration of rise is 5 hours and 5 minutes.
Time zone is 0000.

Below this general list of information the time and height differences are listed.

Time Differences

The first four columns are time differences and are read in the following way:

The first column entry, under High Water: when the time of HW at Dover is 0000 or 1200 UT*, HW at Margate occurs 50 minutes later (+0050).
The second column entry: when the time of HW at Portsmouth is at 0600 or 1800 UT*, HW at Margate occurs 40 minutes later (+0040).
* MHWS tend to occur at the same time in the same place, and the times quoted are for mean spring and neap HWs at Dover. From Fig. 30, spring HWs at Dover are at noon and midnight(ish), neaps are approximately midway between these times.

DOVER
Kent

CHARTS
Admiralty 1698, 1828, 1892; Stanford 1, 9, 19; Imray C8; OS 179
TIDES
0000 Dover; ML 3·7; Duration 0505; Zone 0 (GMT)

Standard Port DOVER (→)

Times				Height (metres)			
HW		LW		MHWS	MHWN	MLWN	MLWS
0000	0600	0100	0700	6·7	5·3	2·0	0·8
1200	1800	1300	1900				

Differences DEAL
+0010	+0020	+0010	+0005	−0·6	−0·3	0·0	0·0

RICHBOROUGH
+0015	+0015	+0030	+0030	−3·4	−2·6	−1·7	−0·7

MARGATE
+0050	+0040	−0010	−0030	−1·9	−1·4	−0·6	−0·3

SHELTER
The small craft anchorage is exposed to winds from NE through S to SW and in gales a heavy sea builds up. Visiting yachts are welcome for up to 14 days. For longer periods, apply in advance. Berthing instructions for Wellington Dock given from Dockmaster's Office at entrance to Granville Dock. Dock gates open, a minimum of HW − 1½ to HW + 1. Waiting pontoon available. Yachtsmen intending to leave the dock should inform the Dockmaster's Office (manned from HW − 2). Small craft may not be left unattended in Outer Harbour.
NAVIGATION
Waypoint from SW 51°06'·15N 01°19'·77E, 180°/000° from/to Admiralty Pier Lt Ho, 0·5M. Waypoint from NE 51°07'·27N 01°21'·51E, 090°/270° from/to S end Eastern Arm, 0·5M. Frequent ferry and hovercraft movements through both entrances. Strong tides across entrances and high walls make entry under sail slow and difficult — use of engine very strongly recommended. Observe traffic signals and follow instructions of harbour patrol launch. Do not pass between buoy marking wreck inside W entrance, Q, and southern breakwater.

Fig. 31 Margate differences.

To calculate the time difference for high water heights other than springs and neaps, the mariner may produce the above information in the form of a graph, or use a little mental arithmetic. Thus, consider the time period 0000 to 0600: the differences are +50 and +40 minutes respectively, and the change from 50 to 40 minutes is assumed to be linear over the six hour period. Therefore when a 0300 morning HW occurs at Dover, the high water at Margate would be 45 minutes later; Fig. 32 is a graphical representation of this.

The calculations for LW differences are carried out in exactly the same way. From the table: when Dover's LW is at 0100 or

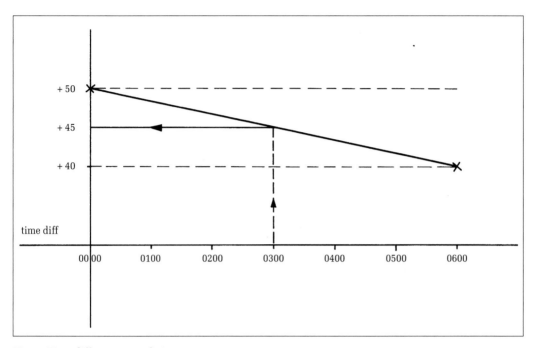

Fig. 32 Time differences graph, Margate.

1300, Margate's LW is 10 minutes earlier (–0010), and it is 30 minutes earlier (–0030) when Dover's LW is at 0700 or 1900. Therefore a Dover LW occurring at 0400 would coincide with a 20 minute earlier tide at Margate.

Height Differences

The next four columns in the secondary port data deal with height differences:

At MHWS Dover (6.7m), the HW at Margate will be 1.9m lower (–1.9). At MHWN Dover (5.3m), the HW at Margate will be 1.4m lower (–1.4).
At MLWN Dover (2.0m), the LW at Dover will be 0.6m lower (–0.6). At MLWS Dover (0.8m), the LW Margate will be 0.3 lower.

Other Differences

Three final thoughts on secondary port difference:

(i) Plotting is not always necessary, and mental arithmetic can produce the interpolation required to find the difference.
(ii) The tide heights quoted in the almanac are mean spring and neap levels, therefore some tides will be higher/lower than those quoted. In such cases the graph line will need to be extended – or the mental effort applied – to obtain the answer by extrapolation.
(iii) In some cases the secondary port's differences are very small, just a few minutes of time or some small decimal fraction of a metre difference in height, and it would not be unreasonable to ignore them.

6

TIDAL STREAMS

The constantly repeating vertical rise and fall of sea water as the tide alternates between HW and LW is supported by a horizontal flow, 'flooding' towards the HW point and 'ebbing away' as the tidal height falls. This horizontal flow is called a 'tidal stream'. In European waters the semi-diurnal tides – that is, two HW and two LW levels each twenty-four hours – give rise to a flow which changes direction at approximately six-hour intervals. The rate of flow varies across the six-hour period: at around both HW and LW times it is almost zero, when the tide is said to 'stand', and at mid-tide it is at a maximum, when the vertical change in height of the rising/falling tide is at a maximum.

Fig. 33 is a repeat of the sinusoidal characteristic curve of a twelve-hour rule tide: the two 'stands' are shown, one at high and one at low water when the change in tidal height around these periods is almost zero, as are the mid-tide periods when the rate of vertical rise or fall of the tide is at a maximum. From this it follows, theoretically, that the flow rate must be almost zero at the times of high and low water, but will be at its fastest at mid-tide periods. In practice, however, the streams are not always slack at times of HW and LW; for example, slack waters

off Dover occur two hours before and four hours after HW.

When planning a passage, particularly along a coast, a prudent skipper will 'work the streams' – that is, he will not, where possible, leave his point of departure until the streams change to flow in the direction of the planned passage; in this way his speed over the ground (SOG) will be the sum of the yacht's speed through the water and the tidal stream. UK tidal steams are typically 0 to 2 knots, and since an average yacht's speed through the water is 4 to 5 knots, a fair tide – one that is going with you – will produce a best SOG of 7 knots; a foul tide, on the other hand, would result in a best SOG of only 3 knots. To ensure a swift passage, the answer of course is to 'work your tides' wherever possible.

In some European waters tidal stream rates are very much greater than the typical 2 knot figure quoted above; this is particularly true at equinoxial spring tides, when very fast tidal streams occur. When a passage is greater than six hours and periods of a foul tide cannot be avoided, it may be advantageous to enter a convenient mid-passage port or to anchor until the turn of the tide, since even simple manoeuvres can become more involved:

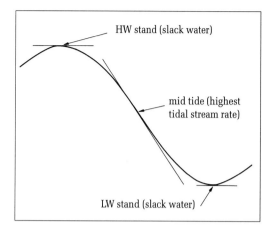

Fig. 33 The twelfths rule.

for instance, entering Yarmouth (IOW) at a mid-spring tide, when the stream runs very quickly across the entrance, can be quite tricky – the yacht will have to be pointed well into the stream to complete the exercise successfully, and it is one of those periods when the reliability of the yacht's engine passes more than briefly through a skipper's mind. Similarly, returning to the UK from the Channel Islands may well include running past Cap de la Hague where spring tide streams of 8 knots can be experienced – clearly, under such extreme conditions the passage round the headland would have to be avoided. Only careful planning and an understanding of the streams will enable a skipper to avoid delays caused by fast foul tides.

When crossing a body of water such as the English Channel where the passage is made at roughly 90 degrees to the streams, their effects will tend to cancel each other out, especially in the case of the Channel when the 60 mile (100km) crossing will take approximately twelve hours: the yacht will simply but safely drift with the stream. Bear in mind, however, that it is much better to arrive at the other side 'uptide' of your destination port, rather than having to fight the tide in order to make your entry. Thus on a sea cruise, plan to use the mid-tide rate to assist you, so that you arrive at your destination at, or near a stand of the tide, because this will make for an easy entry to the destination port.

The hourly direction and speed of the tidal stream, known technically as the 'set and drift' of the tide, are published as a series of chartlets in the various editions of the *Admiralty Tidal Stream Atlas*, and the skipper will have to obtain the atlas covering the particular area of interest – for example, tidal atlases are produced for many separate areas, the English Channel and the Solent being just two of them. Tidal stream data is also shown on charts as a table of 'set and drift' values.

Using the *Admiralty Tidal Stream Atlas*

Fig. 34 is an extract from a tidal stream atlas covering the sea area Littlehampton to Burnham-on-Crouch; this particular atlas is based on the times of high water at Dover. Tidal atlases covering other areas may well be based on a different standard port.

The information shown in Fig. 34 is used in the following way:

1. The time of HW Dover is lightly pencilled in on the HW Dover chartlet. Fig. 34 chartlets cover only the hours before HW Dover, but the full atlas has a complete page for each chartlet and would also cover the hourly intervals after HW

Dover; the relevant ship's time would be lightly printed on each chartlet.

2. On the chartlets the direction arrows indicate by their length, thickness, density and arrowhead the relative strength and direction of the 'set' – that is, the direction in which the tidal stream is running. The two two-digit numbers alongside some of the arrows give the 'drift' – that is, the speed of the stream at that place and at that time. The two digits either side of the separating comma represent the mean neap and spring drift. For example, the arrow and associated figures for the stream off Shoreham, five hours before HW Dover and shown as 08,15, indicate that the stream is running along the coast in an easterly direction, and that the predicted drift at a mean neap tide is 0.8 knots and at mean springs is 1.5 knots (the decimal point is simply not shown on the chartlets). In practice it is convenient to assume that the arrow's data holds true for one full hour, from thirty minutes before the hour stated to thirty minutes after the hour stated.

Examine Fig. 34 again and the chartlet for one hour before HW Dover: the stream off Shoreham is marked as 'slack', indicating that the stream is about to change direction; before this time it is shown going easterly, afterwards it will be shown to be westerly. A skipper wanting to sail east from Shoreham to Eastbourne, a passage of some 24 nautical miles, on a day when the wind forecast will give the yacht an assumed 6 knots through the water, would do well to take advantage of a favourable tide by leaving at, say, five hours before HW Dover, because as can be seen from Fig. 34, the tide is then fair for the journey. Let us assume that on the day in question a spring tide HW at Dover is predicted for 1100 BST. According to the

chartlets, for five hours before HW Dover, covering the period 0600 to 1100 BST, the tide is fair for the complete passage: thus by leaving his berth at this early hour the skipper should be outside the harbour to pick up a favourable stream, giving him a lift of something like 1.5 knots of stream for each hour of the journey. Without a stream, the 24-mile passage at 6 knots would take some four hours; with a favourable stream, however, 6 knots through the water and a stream of 1.5 will give, during the first hour, a ground distance of 7.5 miles, and approximately the same ground coverage for the next two hours would indicate that the yacht should be off Eastbourne in just over three hours. You will see later how a more accurate prediction of a stream-aided passage can be constructed.

In a similar running, but foul tide, the passage would take some five hours to complete.

Charted Tidal Streams

The tidal stream table extracted from chart 5061, Dover to North Foreland, is shown at Fig. 35, the standard port being Dover. To use the table, the left-hand column is entered with the time of HW Dover, or an appropriate hour before or after HW Dover. The top of each column in the table is marked with a 'tidal diamond', each diamond having a capital letter in its centre and an associated lat./long. position. The lat./long. position printed alongside each tidal diamond pinpoints the position on the chart where the set and drift figures in that column of the table apply; the lettered tidal diamond is shown again at the actual position on the chart. The first column for

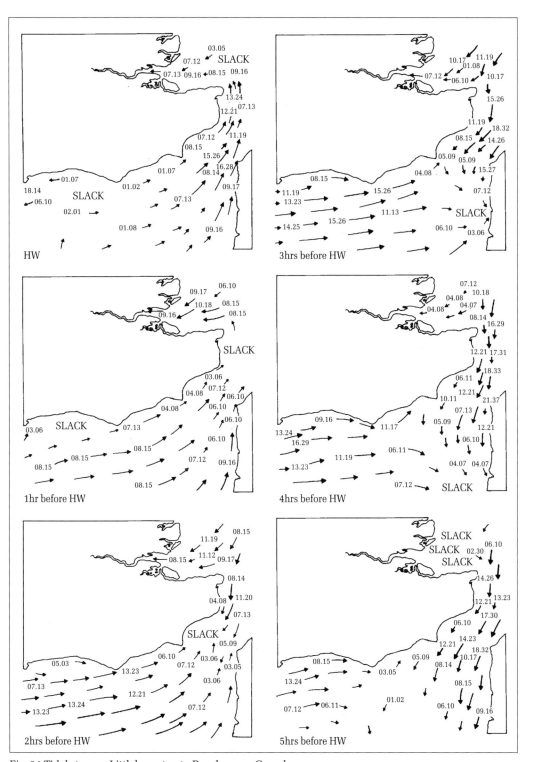

Fig. 34 Tidal streams Littlehampton to Burnham-on-Crouch.

example is tidal diamond A, and its position is 51°23'9N 1°20.5E; entering this column at the HW point gives the set as 250°(T), the spring tide drift 1.7 knots and the neap tide drift 1.1 knots. Therefore at position 51°23'9N 1°20.5E on the chart, the set and drift at the time of HW Dover is 250°(T) at 1.7 knots for a spring tide and 250°(T) at 1.1 knots for a neap tide.

Remember that the 'set direction' is the direction in which the stream is moving; thus a yacht under way but not making way, at this position and time, would be moving over the ground at 250° and at springs would find itself 0.85 n.m. in that direction after 30 minutes.

It is very convenient to assume that the set and drift figures in the table hold good for one hour – that is, from 30 minutes before the printed time to 30 minutes after the printed time: for example, the figures given for HW Dover hold good for the one-hour period HW–30 minutes to HW+30 minutes.

The table in Fig. 35 lists fourteen tidal diamonds, each one representing a position on the chart. A navigator working up a course to steer, or when trying to arrive at an EP (see next chapter) in the vicinity of a tidal diamond, simply extracts the data from the quoted diamond at the relevant time. Remember that the figures given for tidal set and drift are for mean spring and neap rate, and are individually quoted to a specific time and place; in practice, of course, a yacht will spend most of its time sailing between several tidal diamonds, and the yachtsman will need to interpolate the data from the appropriate diamonds. Note,

Tidal Streams referred to HW at DOVER

Each diamond cell lists: Direction of streams (degrees), Rate at spring tides (knots), Rate at neap tides (knots).

Hours	A 51°23'9N 1 20·5E			B 51°20'3N 1 34·3E			C 51°20'1N 1 30·0E			D 51°19'7N 1 27·7E			E 51°18'2N 1 34·4E			F 51°18'2N 1 31·7E		
	Dir	Sp	Np	Dir	Sp	Np	Dir	Sp	Np	Dir	Sp	Np	Dir	Sp	Np	Dir	Sp	Np
−6	064	1·0	0·8	199	2·0	1·2	191	1·0	0·6	203	1·2	0·7	168	1·1	0·6	218	1·1	0·8
−5	070	0·5	0·3	204	2·6	1·6	200	1·5	0·9	203	1·3	0·7	182	1·6	0·9	222	1·7	1·0
−4	239	0·5	0·3	208	3·1	1·7	202	2·0	1·1	210	1·7	1·0	188	2·0	1·1	228	2·3	1·3
−3	250	1·2	0·7	213	2·8	1·5	199	2·2	1·3	208	1·9	1·1	192	2·1	1·2	229	2·1	1·2
−2	250	1·5	0·9	222	1·6	0·8	203	1·7	0·9	215	1·4	0·8	215	0·8	0·4	230	1·2	0·7
−1	250	1·7	1·1	357	0·8	0·5	340	0·6	0·3	005	0·6	0·4	360	1·2	0·7	016	0·6	0·3
0 (HW)	250	1·7	1·1	016	2·5	1·4	007	2·4	1·3	021	2·2	1·2	002	2·4	1·4	039	2·0	1·1
+1	255	0·9	0·6	023	3·2	1·8	016	2·4	1·3	030	2·3	1·3	008	2·1	1·2	044	2·3	1·3
+2	070	0·5	0·3	029	2·9	1·6	023	2·0	1·1	032	1·9	1·1	012	1·4	0·8	045	2·1	1·2
+3	070	1·8	1·1	044	2·2	1·3	031	1·4	0·8	043	1·2	0·7	010	0·8	0·4	048	1·6	0·9
+4	070	1·9	1·2	059	1·2	0·7	061	0·7	0·4	073	0·4	0·2		0·0	0·0	057	0·8	0·5
+5	066	1·5	0·9		0·0	0·0	135	0·4	0·2	195	0·6	0·3	142	0·5	0·3	168	0·4	0·2
+6	065	1·1	0·7	197	1·4	0·8	195	0·8	0·5	203	1·1	0·6	163	0·9	0·6	210	1·0	0·5

Hours	G 51°17'9N 1 29·4E			H 51°16'3N 1 27·4E			I 51°15'2N 1 32·6E			J 51°13'3N 1 26·8E			K 51°13'0N 1 36·4E			L 51°10'5N 1 32·2E			M 51°09'0N 1 27·8E			N 51°08'6N 1 20·4E		
	Dir	Sp	Np	Dir	Sp	Np	Dir	Sp	Np	Dir	Sp	Np	Dir	Sp	Np	Dir	Sp	Np	Dir	Sp	Np	Dir	Sp	Np
−6	206	1·5	0·8	195	2·0	1·1	223	1·9	1·1	181	1·6	0·9	190	0·9	0·5	225	1·7	1·0	212	2·2	1·2	224	2·3	1·3
−5	214	2·1	1·2	197	2·6	1·5	228	2·5	1·4	183	2·1	1·1	191	2·3	1·3	225	2·5	1·4	213	2·2	1·2	231	2·6	1·4
−4	218	2·5	1·4	197	2·8	1·5	228	3·1	1·7	186	2·1	1·2	196	3·1	1·7	222	3·1	1·7	216	1·9	1·1	233	2·4	1·3
−3	217	2·5	1·4	202	2·4	1·3	225	3·1	1·7	188	1·9	1·0	196	3·2	1·8	219	2·9	1·6	228	1·3	0·8	225	1·5	0·8
−2	219	1·5	0·9	215	1·0	0·6	231	1·2	0·7	190	0·8	0·5	195	2·0	1·1	224	1·4	0·8				225	0·3	0·2
−1	008	0·7	0·4	012	1·3	0·7	040	1·3	0·7	007	0·9	0·5		0·0	0·0	014	0·5	0·3	032	1·2	0·7	056	2·3	1·3
0 (HW)	024	2·3	1·3	017	2·7	1·5	041	2·7	1·5	001	2·1	1·2	013	1·3	0·7	040	2·2	1·2	038	2·0	1·2	063	3·9	2·2
+1	029	2·8	1·6	027	3·2	1·7	043	2·8	1·6	001	2·3	1·3	016	2·4	1·4	042	3·0	1·7	039	2·3	1·3	064	4·1	2·3
+2	032	2·5	1·4	018	2·6	1·4	046	2·5	1·4	003	2·3	1·3	014	3·1	1·7	037	2·8	1·6	034	2·2	1·2	066	3·5	1·9
+3	039	1·7	1·0	022	1·7	0·9	049	1·7	1·0	002	1·4	0·8	017	2·6	1·5	047	1·9	1·1	031	1·5	0·8	072	2·6	1·4
+4	050	0·9	0·6	037	0·6	0·3	055	0·7	0·4	017	0·6	0·3	018	1·7	1·0	061	0·9	0·5		0·0	0·0	087	1·3	0·7
+5	156	0·3	0·2	205	0·4	0·2	171	0·2	0·1	161	0·3	0·2	018	0·6	0·3	187	0·3	0·2	203	1·0	0·6	208	1·1	0·6
+6	202	1·1	0·6	197	1·6	0·9	219	1·5	0·9	180	1·3	0·7	189	0·5	0·3	218	1·3	0·7	210	1·8	1·0	220	2·2	1·2

Fig. 35 Tidal stream Dover to North Foreland.

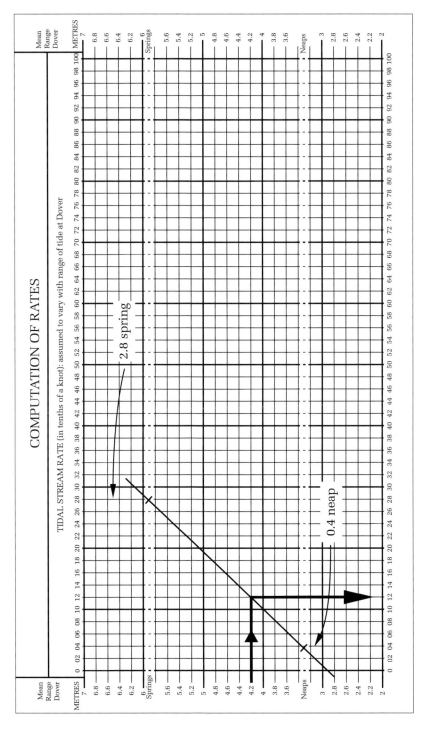

Fig. 36 Computation table.

too, that it is quite pointless trying to be too precise with these figures, or taking them to be accurate; at best you will be left with only an 'estimate' of how the tidal stream will affect your course over the ground.

Example: At a time of neaps, a yacht sailing midway between tidal diamond A and tidal diamond B at a time of Dover HW–3, would extract the following from the table shown in Fig. 35:

Diamond A   set 250°   drift 0.7 knots
Diamond B   set 213°   drift 1.5 knots

Interpolation gives:
set (250–213°)/2+213 = 37°/2+213
$$= 18.5+13 = 241°$$
drift (1.5–0.7)/2+0.7 = 0.8/2+0.7
$$= 1.1 \text{ knots.}$$

This estimated set and drift holds for the hour HW–3.5 to HW–2.5. The stream data obtained from tidal chartlets and chart tables quoted above are for spring and neap tides; to obtain stream figures for periods outside these tides, either the yachtsman must do further mental interpolations, or he should use a 'computation of rates' table such as the one shown at Fig. 36 – in this figure the table is based on HW Dover. the vertical scales are marked off in 'range of tide' and the horizontal

scales in 'tidal stream rates' or drift. Note also that the range of mean neap and mean spring tides for Dover are highlighted by dotted lines across the table, mean spring and neap ranges being 5.9 and 3.3m respectively.

To use the table, the tidal chartlets or the tidal table are first used to get the data for the neap and spring tides drift, say 0.4 and 2.8 knots respectively. These values are plotted against the neap and spring ranges, as shown at Fig. 36, then joined by a straight line. The navigator having calculated the range of the tide for the day, and charted the position of interest, enters this value – say, 4.2m – into the vertical scale of the compilation table, and from where this entry intercepts the drawn line, reads off the tidal drift figure: in this case Fig. 36 yields a rate of 1.2 knots.

When using the compilation table it should be remembered that the neap and spring ranges, shown dotted across it, are calculated from mean values of these tides, and since some spring tide ranges are greater and some neap tide ranges smaller than the mean values, the navigator may well experience a tidal range outside the mean values – in which case the intercept on the drawn line will be an extrapolation and not an interpolation.

The set of the tide is assumed to be that quoted for neap and spring ranges.

7
CHARTWORK 2

In Chapter 4, Chartwork 1, a yacht's position was plotted using only the compass course steered and the logged distance run. The resultant dead reckoning position (DR) is very rarely an accurate one, however, because it does not take into account the sideways movement of the yacht through the water – ie leeway – nor does it allow for tidal set and drift. Leeway is caused because the wind entering the sails of a yacht not only pushes her forward, but also tends to push her downwind at right-angles to her heading. The amount of leeway is dependent upon wind strength, point of sail and the underwater design of the ship's hull; it can be estimated by looking back over the stern of the boat, taking a hand-bearing compass bearing of the yacht's wake and subtracting this value from, or subtracting from it, the reciprocal of the compass bearing – see Fig. 37. Leeway is at a maximum when beating hard to windward, and zero on a full downwind run; it is quoted as being typically 10°, but it will vary from one yacht to another, and the prudent skipper will measure its value whenever he can.

Estimated Position (EP)

A yacht is steered by her compass, and her compass course is the ship's heading – that is, the direction in which she is pointing. The effect of leeway is to push the boat downwind such that her course over the ground – now called her 'wake course' – is the compass course plus or minus the leeway. The effect of leeway on a yacht's movement over the ground is shown at Fig. 37 – notice that the yacht's heading and her course over the ground are not the same.

The tidal set and drift will also affect a yacht's course over the ground ('COG'). Where the tidal set is in the same direction as the yacht's course, her speed over the ground is simply the sum of her speed through the water and the tidal drift; where the set is in the opposite direction, her SOG is equal to her speed through the water minus the tidal drift.

In general the tidal stream set will be at some angle to a yacht's wake course, rather than dead ahead or astern, and its effect then is best seen by constructing a diagram called, technically, a 'vector diagram': see Fig. 38. When constructing such a diagram the navigator is said to be 'working up an estimated position (EP)',

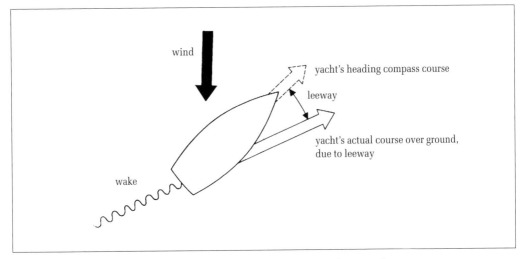

Fig. 37 Leeway – The effect of leeway is to push the yacht sideways, downwind.

and he will usually produce one after each hour's sailing. He does this by first drawing the DR from the last plotted position, line ab; he will then add the wake course line, ac – that is, allowing for leeway – which will have the same length as the ship's DR line and always be downwind of it. Next he will append a line representing the tidal set and drift to the end of the wake course: line cd, technically called the tidal vector. Finally he will add a line joining points a and d: this line represents the course over the ground during the last hour. The construction is annotated by placing identifying arrowheads on each line, a single one on lines ab and ac, two on line ad and three on line cd. An EP takes into account the following:

1. the compass course steered;
2. the logged distance run through the water;
3. the leeway, sideways push of the wind; and
4. the tidal stream, set and drift.

The charted position at the end of the tidal vector is the 'estimated position' (EP) of the yacht; it is marked on the chart by an enclosing triangle, and is annotated with time and log values. Apart from a three-point fix, 'working up' an EP is the most accurate method of plotting a yacht's position without the aid of astro-navigation or electronic plotting. In Fig. 38 the line ad is the COG travelled by the yacht: it is called the ground course.

An EP should be plotted onto the chart at hourly intervals; however, although it is the best that the navigator can do – taking, as it does, all things into account – it is still only an estimated position, and inevitably questions will arise such as: how well has the course been steered? How good was the estimation of leeway? How accurate was the interpretation of the tidal set and drift for the yacht's particular course and position? All will be constantly on the skipper's mind, and verification of the yacht's position is a permanent quest: he will be constantly checking if the echo sounder reading

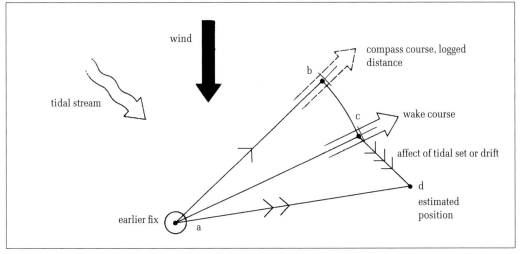

Fig. 38 Plotting an EP.

agrees with the sounding on the chart at the EP; if there are any conspicuous shore features visible which also appear on the chart, or any buoys visible. Ideally everything visible and readable must confirm the EP, and if it doesn't, then the EP is suspect and extra caution is required until the boat's position can be estimated more accurately.

One extremely accurate way of plotting a yacht's position is by taking bearings of conspicuous (shown as 'conspic'), charted shore features and transferring these bearings onto the chart. Ideally three shore objects are required, although two will do – and as we shall see, when necessary a fix can be obtained using only one shore feature.

Three-Point Fix

Good examples of 'conspic' features are church spires, water towers and flagstaffs, the yacht 'must' be somewhere along each one of these three 'position lines'. The reciprocal of each bearing taken is plotted on the chart from each individual shore feature.

It is just possible that the bearings, taken carefully and accurately, will all cross at a point on the chart, that point being the position of the yacht from which the bearings were taken. In practice, accurate bearings are difficult to take from the deck of a sailing yacht, and the lines will most likely enclose a small area known as a 'cocked hat', rather than at a single point. The yacht is assumed to be in the centre of the cocked hat as shown at Fig. 39. If only two charted shore objects can be seen, the crossing of their reciprocal bearings will still indicate the yacht's position; however, the crossing of three over the small cocked hat area gives confirmation that all three bearings are good.

Ideally the three objects should be about 30° to 50° apart to give a good cut on the chart, and they should not be more than 3 to 5 nautical miles away because only a small error in the reading of the

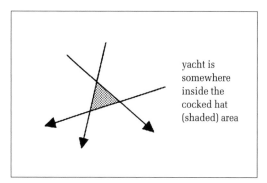

Fig. 39 The cocked hat.

bearing of a distant object will produce a large cocked hat. The bearing of an object on the beam should be taken last, because that object's bearing is altering at the fastest rate.

Finally, the objects of interest should be taken into account first; a crew-mate should jot down their identity, copying the bearings against them as they are called out in an agreed order – note that a modern flux gate compass allows the bearings to be stored as they are taken.

A Running Fix

This method is sometimes called 'doubling the angle on the bow', and it requires only one fixed conspicuous shore object. In order to simplify its construction on the chart we will assume that both leeway and tidal effects are zero.

So, a bearing is taken of the shore object using the hand-bearing compass, and the distance log reading is noted. The reciprocal bearing is plotted on the chart from the shore object such that it cuts the course line, and the resultant 'angle on the bow' is calculated. Fig. 40(i) shows a yacht on course 075°magnetic; using a hand-bearing compass, the bearing of the

shore object was taken as 045°, giving an angle on the bow of 30° (75–45). The passage is continued until the angle on the bow has doubled, in this case becoming 60°. Fig. 40(i) shows that this will be true when the object bears 015° magnetic. It is necessary to pre-calculate this 'doubled angle', here 60°, in order to know what the bearing of the object will be when the bow angle doubles. Once he knows this – here 015° magnetic – the navigator monitors the object until the correct bearing 'comes on'. The distance log is then noted.

Fig. 40(ii) explains how the distance travelled by the yacht between the time of the two bearings is equal to the yacht's distance off the shore object at the time of the second bearing. If the logged distance was 5 knots, then at the time of the second bearing the position of the yacht will have been fixed at a bearing of 195°(M) from the shore object (reciprocal bearing of 015°(M)), a distance of 5 nautical miles.

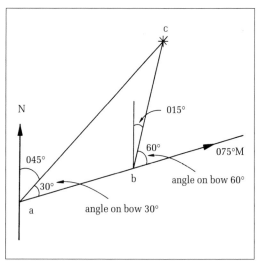

Fig 40(i) Running fix. The logged distance (a–b) is equal to the distance off (b–c).

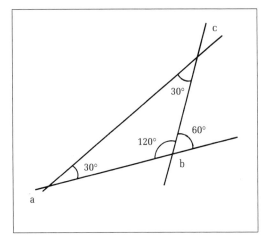

Fig 40(ii) Since the second bearing on the bow is 60° the angle abc must be 30°. In a triangle with two equal internal angles, here 30°, the sides opposite those equal angles are equal in length, therefore line bc, distance off, equals line ab, distance (5nm).

The proof of a running fix lies in the trigonomical truth that in a triangle with two equal internal angles, the sides opposite those angles are equal in length.

Transfer Position Line

This is a second method of fixing a yacht's position with only one shore object in view. In this case we will say that both leeway and tidal effects are present. Assuming the time to be 1200 BST, the following details are noted: the yacht's course is 080°(M), the object's bearing is 030°(M), and the log reading is 685 nautical miles. Fig. 41 shows the situation, the wind being from the north, leeway 10°. At 1300 BST a second bearing is taken, of the same shore object: it is noted as 337°(M), the log 691 nautical miles. From 1200 to 1300 BST the tidal set and drift was 180°(T) at 2.0 knots. In the light of this information we will attempt to calculate the yacht's position at 1300 BST.

The reciprocal of the first bearing is laid off on the chart from the shore object. Assuming that the yacht's passage has so far been in extreme weather conditions and that her plotted position is very suspect, the skipper at least now knows with certainty that the yacht was somewhere on the bearing line at the time it was taken – and it may even be possible to estimate her distance from the shore with the naked eye. Howsoever a point is chosen on the plotted bearing line as the yacht's 1200 hour position, the EP for the next hour is plotted from that point. Thus at 1300 the second bearing is taken and plotted, and Fig. 41 shows what this situation is most likely to be – but there is a problem. The EP should lie on the second bearing line, after all the two bearings were carefully and accurately taken, and the EP very carefully plotted – so where lies this problem?

It originates in the fact that the 1200 hour position on the first bearing line can only be a guesstimate: certainly the yacht must have been somewhere on that first bearing, and it is reasonable to use the planned ground track – however, that can at best only produce an estimated position and is in fact erroneous. But remember, an EP is always estimated. We solve our problem by drawing a new dotted line, parallel to the first bearing line, so that it passes through the EP and cuts the second bearing line: this cut is the 1300 hour position of the yacht. Fig. 41 shows this new line, which in reality is the transferred first position line, as well as the correct 1300 hour position of the yacht. It also shows that if the EP is drawn in reverse order – that is, from the known accurate 1300 hour position – it

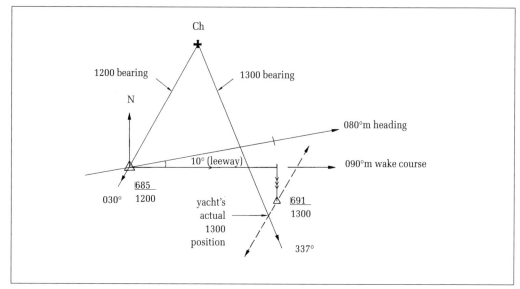

Fig. 41 The transfer position line.

cuts the first bearing at what must have been the yacht's 1200 hour position.

The yacht's position given by the 'closed' triangle, formed by the two bearings and the yacht's plotted ground track, is no more accurate than the EP construction itself; however, it does include an estimation of 'distance off'.

Working up an EP is a navigator's exercise completed 'after the event', because the yacht will have sailed, usually, for at least one hour between plotted EPs. As we have seen, her heading and logged distance may give only a very approximate indication of her position, and in working up an EP the actual ground track during the previous hour is not known until the EP is on the chart. Clearly this will not do, since the navigator must always 'know' the ground track. EPs are necessary and important because it is essential to 'know one's position'; however, before we depart on our passage, or if at any time we change course, we must know what the

ship's heading must be in order to cover a desired ground track, allowing for the estimated leeway and tidal set and drift effects. We gain this knowledge by calculating 'a course to steer'.

Working Out a Course to Steer

In working out such a course, the navigator begins by plotting a faint pencil line between departure and destination points on the chart to ensure that this direct line, the desired ground track, is suitable and safe. Assuming that it is, the following exercise demonstrates the plotting of a course to steer:

The desired objective: a 10 n. mile, 090°T ground track.
Wind and stream conditions: a force 4 northerly wind, the first hour's tidal

stream 180°T at 1.5 knots, the second hour's tidal stream 120°T, at 2 knots. Estimated yacht speed through the water: 5 knots.

1) From the point of departure, point 'a', plot the tidal stream vector for the first hour of the passage – here, 180°T at 1.5 knots, line ab of Fig. 42. Point b would be the position of a yacht lying dead in the water, no sail or engine, after one hour, due entirely to the stream. However, during the hour in question the yacht will have been sailing on a course that will position it on the desired ground track. To plot this course it is necessary to assume an estimated speed through the water, here 5 knots, so that the distance travelled through the water in one hour can be set on the dividers, using the adjacent latitude scale on the chart. Place one point of the dividers on point b of line ab, and with the other point of the dividers make a light mark on the ground track, point c. Pencil in line bc. Line bc represents the course to be steered, from point 'a', making an allowance for tidal set and drift only.

2) Next it is necessary to estimate leeway, and this can only be done with any accuracy by one who knows the boat's behaviour; however, in a good breeze a yacht on a beat will suffer some 10° of leeway – that is, she will be blown downwind by this angle. On a run the leeway will be zero. Here the yacht is on a beam reach, so we will assume 5° of leeway. So now! to consider this leeway, unless we 'lay off' for it, the yacht will be carried downwind of our intended course. To lay off for leeway in our example, plot a third line on our construction detailed in 1) above: line bd, 5° into the wind. Line bd is the course to steer from point 'a' to

ensure that the yacht's ground tack is our original one of 090°. After one hour the yacht will be at position c.

Fig. 42(i) has been completed to show the second hour of the passage and the yacht's position at the end of the two hour period, point 'f'. You will note that the yacht has not travelled exactly 10 n.ms during these two hours – in fact the diagram shows that she will have have gone past her destination to point f. This is because the second hour's tidal stream gave the boat a 'lift' in the right direction. The diagam can be modified to show the time of arrival by drawing a new line, parallel to line ef, cutting through the destination and the second hour's tidal line ce. The diagram is already complex so I have not included this last line; however, take a ruler, and using one centimetre to the nautical mile, apply it to the diagram – you will see it would measure a little under 4 miles. Our ETA is therefore four-fifths of the second hour; the total journey time is 1 hour and 48 minutes.

Fig. 42(ii) is a solution to the same problem, but the two hours' tidal figures have been drawn first, line abc. From c, two hours sailing at 5 knots has been added to touch the desired track at point d, and finally an allowance for leeway has been drawn. Once again we have gone too far in our two hours, but drawing a line parallel to cd and cutting through both destination and tidal line bc will give the correct ETA. *Note* that the term applied is 'estimated position' because:

1) leeway can only be estimated;
2) tidal set and drift can only be estimated;
3) the course actually steered will be a 'rounded' value of the plotted course.

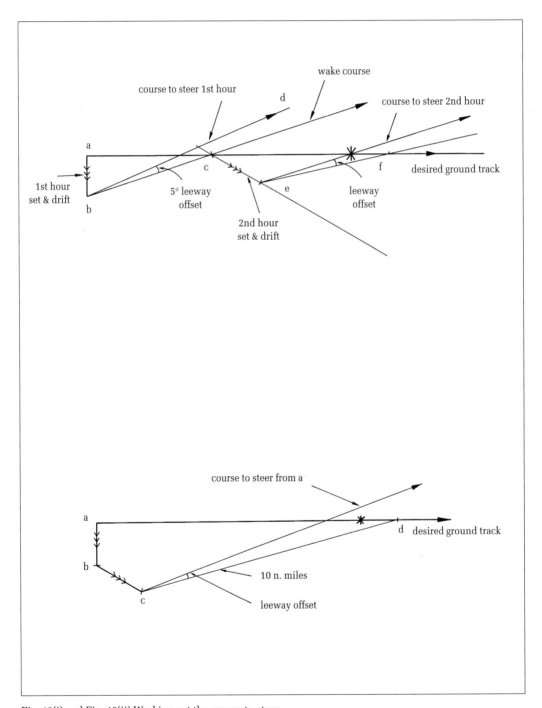

Fig. 42(i) and Fig. 42(ii) Working out the course to steer.

During the passage, noting things such as charted depth, depth contours on passage and transits all help to give confidence in a yacht's position; three-point fixes or a bearing of a charted feature while on a good 'cutting' transit give excellent confirmation, or otherwise. Also be aware that in practice, a yacht may well, for instance, leave her berth and move down-river to the estuary, only to find that the wind will not let her take the course calculated above; this simply means that she must make the best course that she can, with the navigator doing a fast recalculation and plot – the earlier work is not wasted, it has merely concentrated the mind on the problem.

8
BUOYAGE AND LIGHTS

Buoyage for navigation in European waters came into use in the mid-fifteenth century, the first buoys appearing in the Thames estuary in about 1540, although a uniform system of buoyage across all nations was not achieved until the 1970s. Current practice dictates that navigation marks are laid following one of two systems, namely lateral or cardinal. By day it is the shape and colour of buoys which defines the safe water, and by night it is the colour and rhythm of their lights.

The Lateral System

According to this system the buoys mark the port and starboard extremes of a channel or the safe passage along a coast; they are defined as 'port-hand' or starboard-hand' marks, and are laid according to the 'general direction of buoyage'. All charts have this direction clearly defined by means of a large magenta arrow. Vessels travelling in the identified general direction leave port-hand marks to port, and starboard-hand marks to starboard, and those travelling in the opposite direction will do the reverse. However, the navigator needs to be aware that at certain points on a chart the general direction

may be changed: take, for example, Egypt Point on the Isle of Wight, where vessels travelling towards Egypt Point from east or west will follow the defined general direction of buoyage in their respective channels – but if they continue past Egypt Point in their easterly/westerly direction, they will then be travelling against the general direction of buoyage.

Poole Fairway buoy at the entrance to the main channel.

West cardinal mark, the solar panels in clear view.

The Cardinal System

In this system, colour bands, top marks and light rhythms define the safe side of a danger. Only four indicators are used, and they mark the cardinal points of the compass in such a way that a north cardinal marker will always be moored on the north side of a danger, indicating that vessels must pass north of it.

Although a uniform system of buoyage was drawn up by the League of Nations in 1936, not many ratified it before World War II swept all buoyage to oblivion. After the war, many individual national buoyage systems reappeared until some thirty were in use. Following a number of accidents in the English Channel, the International Association of Lighthouse Authorities instigated a simple, unambiguous system known as the IALA Maritime Buoyage System A, and this is now used by maritime countries of north-west Europe. It incorporates both the lateral and cardinal marks, and the general direction of buoyage to which the lateral marks apply follows a clockwise direction around great continental masses; however, as we have said, a chart must be examined to find this direction and any reversals of it.

Five types of mark are defined:

1) lateral marks, indicating the port and starboard limits of a defined channel;
2) cardinal marks, to show the compass cardinal point where safe water lies;
3) isolated danger marks, indicating an individual danger around which all is safe water;
4) safe water marks, indicating safe water all round and at the mark – well, not exactly at the mark because there is a great big buoy there; and finally,
5) special marks, which have no navigational significance, their special designation being usually written in the text area of the chart on which they appear.

South cardinal mark in the Hamble river, Southampton.

Identifying Marks

Lateral Marks

Port-hand markers are red-painted, generally can-shaped buoys; sited in a main channel they are huge, usually solid in form, and lit. The chart will indicate which of such buoys are unlit, and if you don't find them first, they will almost certainly find you. Sometimes a topmark is fitted, and this will be painted red and is can-shaped. In smaller channels, especially 'small boat channels', there may be only a small, red, can-shaped topmark on a pole.

Starboard-hand markers are painted green (sometimes black), and in general are cone-shaped; they may also be quite large, and again are not always lit. Smaller channels may also have their starboard side indicated by 'poled', green, cone-shaped topmarks.

Only red and green lights are used on lateral marks; in fact in system A such colours are used exclusively for such marks.

The light pattern may be of any rhythm: quick flashing, flashing, long flashing, group flashing, occulting or group occulting (see below).

Cardinal Marks

These are pillar- or spar-shaped; in small channels the appropriate topmark may be poled. They are coloured in yellow and black bands, with significant topmarks of double cones – these designate the different markers as follows:

North cardinal marker (NCM): black band on top of bottom yellow band, double-coned topmark; both cones point up (north).

South cardinal marker (SCM): yellow band on top of bottom black band, double-coned topmark; both cones point down (south).

East cardinal marker (ECM): middle yellow band, top and bottom black bands, double-coned topmark; the top cone points up, the bottom cone points down, their bases are together.

West cardinal marker (WCM): middle black band, top and bottom yellow bands, double-coned topmark; their points are together.

Cardinal marks are lit with a white light of the following rhythm:

NCM: very quick, or quick flashing (VQf or Qf) continuously.

ECM: three VQ every 5 seconds or three Q every 10 seconds.

SCM: six VQ every 10 seconds or six Q every 15 seconds; both are followed by a long flash (Lf).

WCM: nine VQ every 10 seconds or nine Q every 15 seconds.

Isolated Danger Marks

A pillar or spar buoy, painted black with one or more horizontal red bands; the topmark is always two black spheres. When lit it is a white light with a group of two flashes.

Safe Water Mark

This may be spherical, pillar or spar in shape, with red and white vertical stripes with a spherical topmark; when lit this may be with an occulting isophase or single long flashing white light every 10 seconds.

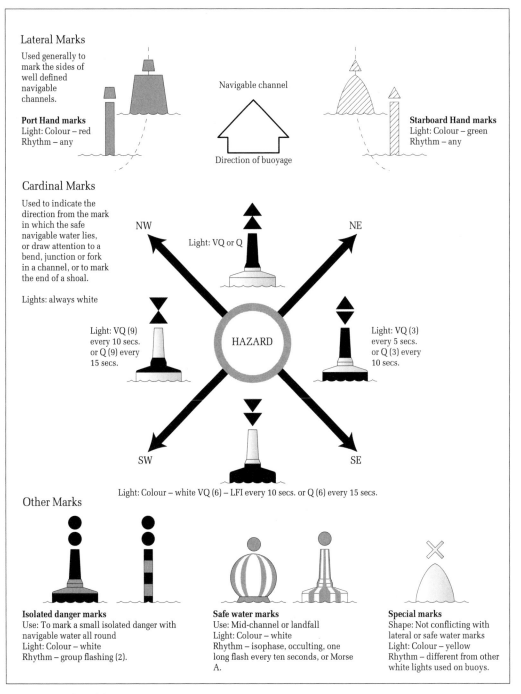

Lateral Marks

Used generally to mark the sides of well defined navigable channels.

Port Hand marks
Light: Colour – red
Rhythm – any

Navigable channel

Direction of buoyage

Starboard Hand marks
Light: Colour – green
Rhythm – any

Cardinal Marks

Used to indicate the direction from the mark in which the safe navigable water lies, or draw attention to a bend, junction or fork in a channel, or to mark the end of a shoal.

Lights: always white

NW

Light: VQ or Q

NE

Light: VQ (9) every 10 secs. or Q (9) every 15 secs.

HAZARD

Light: VQ (3) every 5 secs. or Q (3) every 10 secs.

SW

SE

Light: Colour – white VQ (6) – LFl every 10 secs. or Q (6) every 15 secs.

Other Marks

Isolated danger marks
Use: To mark a small isolated danger with navigable water all round
Light: Colour – white
Rhythm – group flashing (2).

Safe water marks
Use: Mid-channel or landfall
Light: Colour – white
Rhythm – isophase, occulting, one long flash every ten seconds, or Morse A.

Special marks
Shape: Not conflicting with lateral or safe water marks
Light: Colour – yellow
Rhythm – different from other white lights used on buoys.

Fig. 43 Examples of the IALA Maritime Buoyage System A.

Special Marks

These must be yellow, with a yellow top-mark in the form of a cross; the light is also yellow.

Examples of IALA buoys are shown at Fig. 43.

Lighthouses

The lighthouse is a wonderful aid to the navigator, providing a guide to his ship when he is still many miles from land. Beachy Head and Dungeness are just two examples, a very welcome sight to those sailors in UK waters making a night crossing of the English Channel from France. These lighthouses are fully described in the Admiralty list of lights and in the nautical almanacs, and are also briefly described on the appropriate chart. On chart 5055, for example, Beachy Head is highlighted by a magenta star and bubble, and is described as:

Beachy Head Fl(2)20s31m25M
Horn(1)30s.

This may be interpreted as: a white light flashing twice every 20 seconds, the light is 31m above MHWS, and its luminance range is 25 n. miles. It is a white light because white is the default colour; the small 'm' always stands for metres, the capital 'M' for n. miles.

The light is an 'all round' one, although on the chart two obscured arcs are shown; the measurement of the unobscured arc shows that the light illuminates over an arc 248° to 101° (these angles are measured from seaward).

The almanac provides further information, first position which is given as 50°44'.00N 00°14.60E; also that the lighthouse is a white round tower with a red band; and that a fog detector light is fitted showing over an arc 085° to 265°.

Dungeness light is described on the chart as:

Fl.10s40m27M&F.RG.37m11M Fog Det Lt
Horn (3) 60s.

The interpretation of this being: a white light flashing once every 10 seconds, 40m above MHWS, luminance range 27 n. miles; plus a fixed red and green light 37m above MHWS, visible at 11 n. miles; plus a fog detector light; plus a horn sounding three blasts every 60 seconds. The Admiralty list or the nautical almanac would provide more information.

In practice, a yacht approaching from seaward would first be aware of the presence of a lighthouse by the 'loom' of the light as it sweeps across the horizon in an arc which illuminates the sky; the loom may be seen long before the pin-point of the light itself is visible, and it means that a rough bearing may be taken and the corresponding position line drawn. In many instances the loom of two different lighthouses may be visible. The pattern of the loom identifies the individual lighthouses, and the bearings taken from these allow a 'fix' to be plotted on the chart. Eventually the pin-point of light will appear on the horizon, albeit intermittently, and when it does, the navigator can refer to a 'distance off' table such as the one shown at Fig. 44. The table is entered with 'height of eye' against 'height of light', the co-ordinates of which produce the yacht's distance from the light in nautical miles and decimal fractions – for example: a height of eye of 3m

Lights – distance off when rising or dipping (nautical miles)

Height of light		Height of eye									
meters	feet	meters	1	2	3	4	5	6	7	8	9	10
		feet	3	7	10	13	16	20	23	26	30	33
10	33		8.7	9.5	10.2	10.8	11.3	11.7	12.1	12.5	12.8	13.2
12	39		9.3	10.1	10.8	11.4	11.9	12.3	12.7	13.1	13.4	13.8
14	46		9.9	10.7	11.4	12.0	12.5	12.9	13.3	13.7	14.0	14.4
16	53		10.4	11.2	11.9	12.5	13.0	13.4	13.8	14.2	14.5	14.9
18	59		10.9	11.7	12.4	13.0	13.5	13.9	14.3	14.7	15.0	15.4
20	66		11.4	12.2	12.9	13.5	14.0	14.4	14.8	15.2	15.5	15.9
22	72		11.9	12.7	13.4	14.0	14.5	14.9	15.3	15.7	16.0	16.4
24	79		12.3	13.1	13.8	14.4	14.9	15.3	15.7	16.1	16.4	17.0
26	85		12.7	13.5	14.2	14.8	15.3	15.7	16.1	16.5	16.8	17.2
28	92		13.1	13.9	14.6	15.2	15.7	16.1	16.5	16.9	17.2	17.6
30	98		13.5	14.3	15.0	15.6	16.1	16.5	16.9	17.3	17.6	18.0
32	105		13.9	14.7	15.4	16.0	16.6	16.9	17.3	17.7	18.0	18.4
34	112		14.2	15.0	15.7	16.3	16.9	17.2	17.6	18.0	18.3	18.7
36	118		14.6	15.4	16.1	16.7	17.2	17.6	18.0	18.4	18.7	19.1
38	125		14.9	15.7	16.4	17.0	17.5	17.9	18.3	18.7	19.0	19.4
40	131		15.3	16.1	16.8	17.4	17.9	18.3	18.7	19.1	19.4	19.8
42	138		15.6	16.4	17.1	17.7	18.2	18.6	19.0	19.4	19.7	20.1
44	144		15.9	16.7	17.4	18.0	18.5	18.9	19.3	19.7	20.0	20.4
46	151		16.2	17.0	17.7	18.3	18.8	19.2	19.6	20.0	20.3	20.7
48	157		16.5	17.3	18.0	18.6	19.1	19.5	19.9	20.3	20.6	21.0
50	164		16.8	17.6	18.3	18.9	19.4	19.8	20.2	20.6	20.9	21.3
55	180		17.5	18.3	19.0	19.6	20.1	20.5	20.9	21.3	21.6	22.0
60	197		18.2	19.0	19.7	20.6	20.8	21.2	21.6	22.0	22.3	22.7
65	213		18.9	19.7	20.4	21.0	21.5	21.9	22.3	22.7	23.0	23.4
70	230		19.5	20.3	21.0	21.6	22.1	22.5	22.9	23.2	23.6	24.0
75	246		20.1	20.9	21.6	22.2	22.7	23.1	23.5	23.9	24.2	24.8
80	262		20.7	21.5	22.2	22.8	23.3	23.7	24.1	24.5	24.8	25.2
85	279		21.3	22.1	22.8	23.4	23.9	24.3	24.7	25.1	25.4	25.8
90	295		21.8	22.6	23.3	23.9	24.4	24.8	25.2	25.6	25.9	26.3
95	312		22.4	23.2	23.9	24.5	25.0	25.4	25.8	26.2	26.5	26.9
metres	feet	metres	1	2	3	4	5	6	7	8	9	10
		feet	3	7	10	13	16	20	23	26	30	33
Height of light					**Height of eye**							

Fig. 44 'Distance off' table.

and a height of light of 32m yields 15.4 n. miles as the distance off. The wise navigator will interpret this as *approximately* 15.4 n. miles.

9

PILOTAGE AND PASSAGE PLANNING

Pilotage describes the safe passage of a vessel or yacht from a port of departure to a port of arrival, and is generally achieved via a consummate knowledge of boat handling, chartwork, compass and distance log – in fact it calls upon the full range of skills known to the experienced sailor. Such passages have undoubtedly been undertaken by complete novices, because after all, as long as you can afford to buy or charter a yacht, there is nothing to stop you – I have even heard of people taking mirror dinghies across the English Channel. However, the success of these ventures is an indication of the Almighty's tolerance, the perpetrators arriving safely by sheer good fortune.

All those who contemplate taking a vessel to sea should first get some training. In this country the RYA arranges a full range of theoretical courses, usually offered at local technical colleges, and a whole host of sailing schools run practical training courses to complement the theoretical ones. The RYA's view on training seems to be that educating sailors is better than legislating them, and who could possibly argue with that. One example of foreign legislation is that all offshore yachts must (shall) carry a six-person liferaft, which seems reasonable enough until you consider an elderly couple who sail together and who would almost certainly be incapable of lifting such a relatively heavy object. The problem with legislation is that its rules are generally too universal, leading to intolerant and often hidebound interpretation.

In contemplating leaving a safe berth, a skipper must be quite sure that both yacht and crew are capable of making the proposed voyage; and if they are, then his overriding concern throughout the trip must be the yacht's position. It goes without saying, I hope, that the passage would only start under favourable weather conditions.

Three- and five-day weather forecasts are now available by telephone or by fax, and this facility should be used. The outline planning of a coastwise passage should always include the 'openness' of ports – that is, whether entry and departure are possible at all states of the tide. And if they are not, then the 'time windows' of access should be established.

To obtain a 'time of passage' certain questions need to be considered; for instance, the total distance or the distance to be run each day; the anticipated speed through the water in the prevailing wind conditions; and whether the tidal streams are favourable or foul. And if the weather were to turn nasty, what 'bolt holes' would be available? Also, there should be large-scale charts of all possible locations on board, and if there are not, the skipper should establish exactly how much detail is available from pilot books or from the chartlets listed in the nautical almanacs. Assuming a shortish passage, are both the departure and destination ports shown on one chart? This is not an essential requirement since transfers from one chart to another are easily made – however, where such transfers are contemplated, the person doing the transfer must pay particular attention to any change of chart scales.

Being able to see the passage from start to finish will allow the skipper to ensure that all navigation hazards are a safe, reasonable distance from the proposed plotted ground track; he will also be able to list, in sequence, all the buoyage and lighthouse details on the route – and a really prudent skipper would also list the course and distance between each navigation mark, because however favourable the starting weather may be, it can so easily turn nasty, with visibility reducing to a few metres. All conspicuous land features such as towers, coastguard stations, hotels, churches, measured-mile poles and charted transits should be noted, and these notes contained in a plastic folder where they can be immediately and continuously available in the cockpit; this means that the helm has passage information immediately available, also that the navigator can spend as much time on deck as necessary, observing transits, buoys and soundings in order to confirm that the desired ground track is being made.

A distance of 50 n. miles or more will entail some night-time sailing. I personally enjoy such activity because the

Entering Granville, France. The 'goal posts' mark the entrance to the harbour.

whole scene changes – navigation marks appear as a line, or as two lines of port and starboard coded light signals, lighthouses flash out their identity, and all surrounding vessels identify their right of passage by coded 'priority lights'. In fact it may be claimed that by arranging to arrive at the distant destination as dawn breaks, identification of that port is made all the easier by the buoyaged light patterns, with final entry completed in daylight. Besides, the romance of such a trip is well worth the loss of sleep – although not every night please! Having said this, it is important that a crew has the confidence to waken their skipper should they feel in any way uncomfortable with the situation. Night-time sailing may involve a reduced cockpit crew of perhaps little experience on watch, and therefore in charge of the boat in the quiet hours when the skipper is snatching some sleep – he cannot do everything, and a certain amount of delegation is unavoidable, especially on long trips. And assuming that not every member of every crew is experienced, some training must take place on each voyage. Even so, the skipper must always be aware that the safety of both crew and boat remain entirely his responsibility even when he is asleep.

Planning and Pilotage, UK to France

This particular passage was undertaken by three friends on a 39ft yacht, and is used here to illustrate some of the points mentioned above. The initial plan was to sail from Plymouth to L'Aberwrach on the north coast of Brittany, a distance to go of approximately 100 n. miles, to be under-taken in predicted fine weather, with north-westerlies of force 3 to 4. At an expected 5 knots it was assumed that the run would take twenty hours, and so the boat was victualled for four days of good eating, with emergency food stores of soup, corned beef and dry biscuits. The two capacious fresh-water tanks were filled, and one of them isolated so that a 50 per cent usage marker existed. Medicinal spirits and wine were carried to help enliven any official merriment, and a 50 litre plastic container of fresh water was also stowed. The fuel tank was filled to capacity, and a second, well marked 50 litre container of diesel was also carried. Two full gas cylinders, and oil for the engine were checked and stowed in the big cockpit locker.

Our yacht belonged to a well run sail training club so that such things as first-aid kit, engine spares, life-raft, buoyancy aids, tools, navigation and safety equipment were on board and needed only to be checked off against the yacht's inventory. The yacht itself was also well used, not the least by the three people contemplating this proposed trip; consequently we did not need any kind of warm-up run in the adjacent coastal waters to get used to her fittings, sails or sailing behaviour.

Even though the journey was expected to take less than two days, we did instigate a watch-keeping system of two hours on and four off, and this was implemented from the time of departure.

We left our berth at the Mayflower Marina (Plymouth) at 1810 on Saturday 16 August; the forecast was variable 3, dying during the night, the line of sight course 190°T, and the distance 100 n. miles, under engine at 5 sustainable knots giving some twenty hours of travel. Reference to the yachtsman's tidal atlas, namely the western approaches and Channel west, gave the following stream detail based on HW Cherbourg:

HW(16th) 1813 5.9m	HW(17th) 0644 5.9m	HW(17th) 1904 6.3m
1813 sl.*	0244 1.6 ➔	1144 0.8 ➔
1913 sl.	0344 1.4 ➔	1304 1.2 ➔
2013 0.3 ⇐	0444 1.2 ➔	1404 2.0 ➔
2113 0.8 ⇐	0544 0.4 ➔	
2213 0.8 ⇐	0644 1.0 ⇐	
2313 0.8 ⇐	0744 1.0 ⇐	
0013 0.2 ⇐	0844 2.0 ⇐	*slack water
0044 sl.	0944 1.6 ⇐	
0144 1.0 ➔	1044 1.0 ⇐	

Over the expected twenty hours the streams therefore approximately cancel each other, and our course 'eyeball' becomes our desired ground track: allowing for variation and zero deviation, our compass course Plymouth to L'Aberwrach was 195°C.

Having passed through the west exit of Plymouth's breakwater, a bearing of the Eddystone light, taken at 2015 and read as 295°M, was plotted, helping to confirm our DR chartwork; log reading was 11.58 n. miles.

During the night Decca fixes and DR plots were charted, as shown below:

Time	Decca position	DR position
0200	not taken	log 44.5:
0600	49°13'N 4°18'W	log 67.0:
		49°13'N 4°28'W
0800	49°03'N 4°18'W	log 78.2:
		48°59'N 4°31.5'W

It was decided at 0800 that, since the stream was now running westerly and our position by Decca was east of our desired track, we would alter course to 205°C. We had approximately 20 n. miles to run, and

this new course would leave us 'uptide' on our arrival off L'Aberwrach.

At 1035 the Ile Vierge lighthouse, 77m 27M, was spotted dead ahead.

At 1200 the WCM Lizen Ven Qust buoy was off to starboard. Course was altered to 230°C to clear Le Lebenter rocks.

At 1300 we rounded WCM Libenter into the Grand Chenal leading marks at 100°T.

At 1350 we moored on L'Aberwrach pontoons.

During the 1200–1300 period very fast streams were experienced, and we had to take clearing bearings on Ile Vierge and Libenter to keep us on course and off the rocks.

Monday 18 August, L'Aberwrach towards Roscoff

The standard port for Roscoff is Brest. Reference to the almanac reveals that Roscoff dries, access is HW ±2 and shelter is good except in strong N. and E. winds; the distance to run is 32 n.miles.

Brest	HW 0432 +6.9m	1655 7.3 m
Diff. Ros.	+ 0100 +1.9m	+0100 +1.9
Roscoff	0532 8.8m	1755 9.2m

Therefore evening tide access was possible at 1755 ± 2 = 1555 to 1955.

A zero wind strength was forecast. The engine was set for 6 knots, anticipating a passage of five hours. We departed at 1400. The weather was very misty, the leading marks only just visible, however pilotage using Libenter, Lizen Ven Quest and Aman ar Ross buoys got us safely out into deep water.

There are some very shallow areas between Ile de Batz and Roscoff, and for this reason, and because Roscoff is at the eastern end of the channel, it was decided to go north of the island. The following GPS waypoints were set to give good clearances:

WP1	48°46'.28N 3°59'.72W
WP2	48°44'.08N 3°57'.04W
WP3	48°44'.01N 3°57'.04W
WP4	48°43'.75N 3°58'.43W
WP5	48°43'.45N 3°58'.60W

WP5 is a point inside Roscoff harbour.

The passage around the north of the island was uneventful, although the waypoint working and GPS route information indicated very strong and changeable tidal streams; without GPS and in poor visibility it would have been prudent to have given the north coast of Ile de Batz a much bigger clearance.

We arrived off Roscoff at 1830,and the harbourmaster directed us to go alongside the south wall of the harbour where we would dry out safely. When at a drying berth the boat should be so balanced that as she hits the bottom she has a slight lean towards and against the wall. We were moored port side to, and under our wise and knowledgeable (he may read this) skipper, the anchor and chain where laid out on the port side-deck; observation from the shore side indicated that we had a slight but sufficient tilt to port, and in the event our yacht touched bottom in an almost upright and therefore comfortable position.

We refloated at 0500 local time, and departed towards Treguier at 0810. The total distance was 41 n. miles, our passage broken at Tregastel Bay, the weather again misty and with only a little wind. Three waypoints were set for the 17 n. miles to the bay, and the passage was uneventful; we entered the bay by leading

marks at 149°T, the channel clearly marked by port and starboard beacons, and dropped anchor in 3.4m at 1500.

We departed for Treguier at 1600, the distance to go 24 n. miles. With waypoint navigation under engine, we arrived off the entrance at the Basse Crublent mark in the early evening: leading marks on 137° down the Grande Passe, changed to 220°T at Pt. Pen Guezec green buoy, thence down a well marked but twisting channel to the marina.

On Thursday 21 August we departed Treguier and made towards St Malo, a distance of 60 n. miles, with an overnight stop at Binic, some 27 n. miles from Treguier.

Departed Treguier 1010; pilotage to the La Corne light tower 48°51'.4N 03°10'.73W, then course 065° to get buoys La Moise (11 n. miles) and La Vieille du Treou in transit. Changed course to 135°M to pass Les Sirlots (15 n. miles) and next ECM at position 48°51'.7N 2°57'.5W to starboard. Waypoints had been set at:

WP1	48°54'.00N 2°59'.00W
WP2	48°51'.09N 2°57'.02W
WP3	48°41'N 2°48'.4W
	(this WP is just off Binic)

The final passage on this trip that will be described here is of Binic to St Malo. It was undertaken in overcast and misty weather, and so as a principle of good seamanship – and just in case – a very detailed passage plan was made, as follows:

WP1	48°39'.02N 2°38'.00W
	(N. of ECM) 7.8 n. miles
WP2	48°41'.74N 2°31'.04W
	(N. of NCM) 5.0 n. miles

WP3   48°41'.74N 2°19'.03W
          (N.of Cap Frethd) 8 n. miles
WP4   48°40'.06N 2°11'.02W
          (N. Green Lateral) 5.4 n. miles
WP5   48°40'.02N 2°07'.50W
          (2.6 n. miles S. of fairway buoy)

Then:

089°T towards Le Grand Jardin lighthouse
No. 4 red bell buoy close to port
No. 6 red buoy good 100m to port
No. 1 green whistle buoy close to starboard
Then S. of E. to leave Le Sou ECM to starboard
Then SE into buoyed channel

The Bas Sablons marina has a cill 2m above CD.

On Saturday 23 August:
St Malo HW 2242 11.7m LW 1720 2.0m
Since our yacht draws 2.2m we needed a rise of tide of exactly this value. Using the tidal curve in the almanac produced LW +2.2m at LW +1.5 hours, meaning we could enter at 1720+0130=1850 (and since French summer time applied, 1950 local time).

Binic is a locked port with access HW ±3. It is a secondary port to St Malo and on the day, HW–3 occurred at 1022 LMT; the distance to run being 33 n. miles, at say 5 knots, gave a passage time of 5.5 hours, with ETA at St Malo of 1352 LMT. We therefore had a large time-window in which to leave Binic for open access to the marina at St Malo.

The above planning may seem excessive to some readers: however, the weather was generally misty with little wind, and the coast was relatively unknown to all the crew; and perhaps just as important, studying before departure the local navigation marks and also the distances to go, helps to concentrate the mind. Moreover, by copying these details onto a waterproof sheet, such local information was constantly and immediately available in the cockpit. The two week passage was completed via the port of Granville, the Channel Islands and Cherbourg, all of which needed similar pilotage details; then we planned the return passage to the UK.

10

ELECTRONIC INSTRUMENTS

Until recently the electronics on a cruising yacht were confined to a 'stand alone' VHF radio, an echo-sounder and a distance log; in more recent years, however, Decca navigation and the global position system (GPS) have become increasingly common, with high resolution radar an attractive addition.

VHF Radio

The range of this equipment, ship to ship, is perhaps 10 n. miles; ship to shore it is perhaps 30 n. miles; and its principle aim is 'safety of life at sea' (SOLAS): basically this means that it is responsible for the making and receiving of distress, urgency and safety radiotelephony traffic on channel 16. It also has the very useful facility of being able to make an initial call to coast radio stations – although it should be noted that these are now called on a working frequency and *not* channel 16 – and other vessels. The system of use follows a strict procedure, and a user must be trained and qualified, or at least under the supervision of a qualified person.

Echo-sounder

This is an electronic transducer which transmits pulses of sonar frequency: these echo back from the seabed to the device's receiver, and the time between transmission and reception is measured, and converted to depth below the transducer. This information is displayed, at the user's discretion, in metres, fathoms or feet, and the depth reading may be offset to give depth below the keel or the depth of water. Minimum and maximum depth alarms can be set. The minimum alarm is quite useful when approaching an anchorage looking for the correct depth in which to drop the hook for an overnight stay.

Distance Log

This log is an underwater impeller or a completely electronic transducer fitted below the hull which allows the boat's speed through the water to be calculated. From this information the log provides switched read-outs of the total distance run since fitting; the distance since it was last switched on; and the speed through the water – there are usually two switch positions for this value, one being more 'damped' – ie steadier – than the other.

Decca Navigator

Decca is a hyperbolic navigation system, that is, a system in which a shore-based master transmitter and up to three slave stations transmit radiowaves which are received by the vessel and compared. The time taken for a radiowave to reach a remote point is a constant, consequently the difference in time between the arrival of the master signal and the signal from each slave in turn can be measured, and this means that the actual difference in range between the master and each slave can be calculated. If all the points having the same difference between master and slave are joined together, three hyperbolic curves will be produced: these are position lines, and the vessel must be at the point where they cross. This calculated point is now usually displayed as latitude and longitude.

GPS

In this satellite navigation system, several satellites are 'visible' to the receiver at any one time. Each satellite transmits its position and its time of transmission, the receiver notes the time of reception, and is then able to calculate the signal transit time and therefore the distance from each satellite. Each of these distances forms a small circle, strictly speaking a position circle, and since the receiving vessel must be somewhere on each circle, its exact position can be assumed to be at the point of their intersection.

Both Decca and GPS are subject to errors which can amount to several hundred metres, so once again it is important to appreciate that such devices, however remarkable they might appear to be, should only ever be treated as a navigation *aid*.

Radar

Essentially radar is a system whereby very short pulses of radio energy are transmitted from a rotating aerial; these pulses travel at very high speeds and are reflected back to the aerial which rotates relatively slowly. The difference in time between transmission and reception is measured, converted into distance off, and displayed on a 'plan position indicating' (PPI) screen. A PPI has a circular display, the centre of which is the vessel itself. A trace rotating about the centre of the display, synchronized to the rotating aerial, displays a spot(s) indicating distance off and bearing from the vessel or object(s) causing the reflection. But *beware*: one *serious* disadvantage concerning radar is that it will *not* show low-lying shorelines, and navigators must realize that an echo from landwards may well be a reflection from relatively high land lying some distance inshore.

The beauty of radar is that it will point out any vessel in your immediate area, the shape of the display spot – a tadpole – giving an indication of its course. Especially those great big yacht-seeking ones that only come out in fog...

Modern Electronic Systems

There is now a splendid array of electronic navigation equipment available to the sailor, so much so that it is often difficult to know what to choose – in spite of claims made by individual manufacturers. The most significant development is that nowadays many manufacturers produce a compatible range of instruments: radars, electronic charts, speed/log, depth, wind and steering instruments, all of matching design and colour. However, the most remarkable thing about them – or so it seems to me – is that although they may still be used as individual stand-alone instruments, as they always have been, they may also be interconnected over a single wire so that each instrument, still under its own microprocessor control but using an internationally recognized protocol, can share the data stored in its individual transducer with any other connected compatible instrument.

A modern high resolution radar set, for example, now has a minimum range of 0.125th of a n. mile, it can discriminate between objects only 23m (75ft) apart, and range markers and bearing lines are available, and under the user's control. Also available are off-centre viewing for greater range in one direction, and zoom facilities, allowing a particular area to be magnified.

Electronic Cartography

In this system 35cm (14in), eight-colour monitors with micro-cartridges are used: these display selected charts, exactly as do the older paper versions, only in this case your vessel is at the centre of the screen, and the charted features simply scroll past you; the chart scales are selectable. By connecting these two instruments together over the single-wire, digital nmea standard communications link, together with such things as digital GPS, depth, speed, wind and compass instruments, the navigator's picture of his surroundings changes quite dramatically. For example, the stand-alone radar display, now gathering extra information from the highway, can be toggled between radar picture and electronic chart, in inset or full display mode; waypoints can be shown, and text windows can be opened to show latitude and longitude, bearing and distance to waypoint or cursor, together with the 'time to go' (TTG) to the next waypoint.

The track of other vessels in the area can be shown, with their course, bearing, speed, range and 'closest point of approach'. The display can be 'north up', 'heading up' or 'course up'.

The radar cursor can be placed on a radar image, and the system toggled to an electronic chart to reveal whether the reflected image is, or is not, a charted feature such as a buoy – and if it is, a text message can be shown giving its position and navigational details. Such systems can store 1,000 waypoints, 1,000 markers and 5,000 trackmarks all on one memory cartridge.

Autopilots

An autopilot will give rudder position and cross-track error (CTE), and the auto system keeps you *on* course; if you want to *change* course, then it is necessary to switch to a manually operated rotary knob or joystick. Such a system will be very accurately laid out on a large, clear, liquid-crystal display (LCD).

A 'man-overboard' (MOB) facility is also available, whereby a pushed button records the position of the MOB, together with a 'return to the spot' course and distance.

New Digital Instruments

Many of these instruments are also inter-connectable across the highway, their display capability making the sailor's life much easier. However, I would still put my head up now and again for a good seamanlike look all around! They might include the following:

Speed/log: giving current speed; average speed; maximum speed; and velocity made good to windward (VMG).

Depth sounders: giving water depth; trend indication; shallow and deep alarm; and anchor watch.

Wind instruments: giving apparent wind, angle and speed; close-hauled segment; maximum wind speed; true wind speed; and steering compass. The display is a heading reference instead of the traditional compass card; it also gives a digital compass read-out, off-course steering indication and a reciprocal course.

New instruments are available for use with traditional paper charts, such as the '**maritime mouse**'. A chart is attached to an electronic mat laid out on the table as normal, and the 'mouse' – a hand-held instrument with LCD read-out – is moved across it. The mouse is linked to a GPS system; it has a clear transparent window with a hole in the centre of it, through which a pencil may be inserted in order to mark a position on the chart. The system needs to be referenced to the chart in use – this takes only a few seconds to complete – after which the mouse updates its position as it is moved across the chart. Four lights equi-spaced around the transparent window indicate the direction to a wanted location.

11

GLOBAL MARITIME DISTRESS
AND SAFETY SYSTEMS

This is a new network of radio and satellite systems designed to enhance the existing operations of 'safety of life at sea' (SOLAS). It consists of a new 'digital selective calling' system (DSC), and is used in conjunction with the current marine radio systems and two satellite systems.

The emphasis of rescue organization has changed, from one where 'ships in the area' were primarily responsible for acknowledging distress calls and making any subsequent rescue, to one in which a fully operational shore-based 'Rescue Coordination Centre' (RCC) automatically responds and controls the rescue by all appropriate means.

'Digital selective calling' may seem an obscure name until it is explained: it is called 'digital' because the system is based on a binary-coded signal unique to each vessel, transmitted at the touch of a button; the button is in some way mechanically protected so that the action of pressing it is a deliberate one. It is 'selective' because a coast radio station can transmit DSC signals to a selected ship or group of ships, or to all vessels in a selected area. Finally, 'calling' describes the means by which a vessel makes the initial, automatic call contact with a coast radio for the purpose of declaring distress or urgency, or for making safety or general radio communication; it is also the means of making an initial call to another vessel for inter-ship communication.

But it is much more than that, too: DSC is fully automated in that the DSC call, automatically transmitted at the touch of the special button, not only identifies the vessel, it can also be programmed to give the vessel's position, and where appropriate, the nature of the distress. Furthermore, whilst it maintains a continuous watch at the coast radio station, it will respond automatically to the received signal by transmitting a DSC 'acknowledge signal'; this in turn initiates three things:

1) it stops any further transmission from the ship's DSC equipment which made the initial call;
2) it tunes the ship's associated radiotelephone (R/T) transmitter/receiver (transceiver) to an appropriate channel ready for communications to continue using voice;
3) it rings a bell and/or switches on a warning light on the ship's equipment.

In fact the ship's equipment will continue to retransmit the initial call until either it receives the 'acknowledge' signal, or it is manually switched off.

The automatic nature of DSC, particularly for vessels in trouble, must be welcomed with open arms, especially by yachtsmen. Several skippers who have had a yacht go down under them and have lived to tell the tale, have talked of the speed with which their entire world disappeared beneath the waves – from initial collision and 'What the...!' to finding themselves alone in the water taking but a few minutes. The current system of 'all voice' distress call and traffic takes some minutes to complete – even the initial call is time-consuming, especially when your only thoughts are getting people off the sinking vessel and into the liferaft. Under the new scheme one press on the button is all that is required.

At this point I feel it is important to emphasize that the response to the button is *automatic, immediate* and will generate a *massive rescue operation*. SO IF YOU PRESS IT WHEN YOU DID NOT MEAN TO – don't just turn it off, because the call will undoubtedly have been heard, and your 'turning off' action will be interpreted as a lost boat. We will deal with an accidental pressing later in this chapter.

Division of the GMDSS System

The GMDSS system divides the oceans of the world into four areas, each being defined by the nominal range of terrestrial radio or satellite communications systems.

Area A1

This is the area around continental land masses where VHF communication is reasonably reliable between vessels at sea and shore radio stations. Vessels within this area will be in range of at least one coast radio station in which continuous DSC alerting is available. However, note that VHF radio signals are in the frequency band 30 to 300 MHz, and because these frequencies travel in a straight line from the transmitter, receiving aerials 'below' the horizon cannot 'see' them and are therefore out of VHF range.

The seaward extent of the VHF area cannot be precisely defined; it is, however, a function of aerial height, and since a coast radio station's aerials are normally sited on the top of headlands, it is usually taken to be 30 n. miles. It is perhaps worth noting here that yacht to yacht VHF range is nominally 15 n. miles.

Area A2

This area excludes area A1. It is in the radio communication range of a medium frequency (MF) coast radio station transmitter, operating in the frequency band 2 to 3 MHz in which continuous DSC alerting is available. Once again the precise seaward extent of this range cannot be defined; however, radio frequency transmissions in this band tend to hug the earth – they are referred to as 'ground wave' transmission frequencies, and are 'seen' by ship receiver aerials below the horizon. The nominal seaward range is 200 to 300 n. miles.

Area A3

This area excludes areas A1 and A2; world wide, it is covered by the 'International Maritime Satellite' system (Inmarsat). In this system, four geostationary satellites provide continuous global alerting between latitudes 70° north and 70° south.

A yacht equipped with an Inmarsat station would normally be fitted with an Inmarsat-C system because of its simple omnidirectional aerial. The ship station itself does not handle voice communications: it is a message system comprising a transceiver, a VDU, a keyboard and a printer.

Area A4

This is the area outside A1, A2 and A3; it is covered by Cospas-Sarsat ('search and rescue' satellite(s)). The polar orbit of these four satellites, together with the earth's rotation about its own axis, ensures that each satellite monitors the entire globe. The 406 MHz EPIRB is the yachtsman's beacon for Cospas-Sart: distress, search and rescue.

Coastal yachtsmen will be mainly interested in carrying the DSC VHF transceiver for on-board distress alerting, and the 406 MHz EPIRB for life-raft distress signals.

VHF DSC Operation

Most yachts now carry a VHF transceiver operating in the frequency range 156–174 MHz. Communications between ship-shore and ship-ship is by radiotelephony, in which an oral/aural link is established.

The frequency band is divided into a number of channels, all of which have some specific use. For example, channel 16 is reserved for distress, urgency, safety, and initial calling to another vessel where a prior arrangement of 'A listening out for my traffic channel' has not been organized between you. Coastal radio stations maintain a constant watch on channel 16. Where a vessel requires to communicate with a shore radio station for any other traffic purpose – for example, a telephone link call – the initial call to that station would be on one of its 'working channels'. Reference to a nautical almanac will reveal the working channel(s) of all UK coast radio stations.

When VHF DSC becomes fully operational the continuous watch on 16 by coast radio stations will cease, although I personally believe that this cessation will not occur for some years to come; however, it is the current intention, and we should prepare for it. In this respect there are two things the yachtsman will have to do: he will have to buy a VHF DSC 'add-on' conversion package which will update his current VHF transceiver – though he could wait until a 'single unit' VHF DSC transceiver became available on the market; and he will have to study for and obtain the 'short range certificate'.

Digital Selective Calling (DSC)

When he obtains a DSC VHF transceiver the yachtsman will be registered with the GMDSS system and, very importantly, will be allocated a unique 'Maritime Mobile Service Identity' number (MMSI). This number will be 'programmed' into the equipment, to the effect that whenever the set initiates a DSC alert, the receiving shore station will be able to identify the sender.

Channel 70 (VHF) is wholly reserved for DSC, and must not, on any account, be used for any other purpose.

When a vessel is in distress – that is, in grave and imminent danger and requiring immediate assistance (inclusive now of man overboard) – pressing the magic button will transmit the DSC alert on channel 70, giving the vessel's identity, plus her position and the time at that position, together with the nature of her distress. The nature of the distress will be selectable from a menu including such things as fire or explosion, flooding, disablement, collision, piracy, man overboard, and undesignated. The transmission will take only fractions of a second and will be repeated automatically every three to four minutes.

The transmissions will cease upon the fulfilment of one of the following:
1) as soon as a DSC 'acknowledge' signal is received;
2) if the ship's operator manually cancels the transmission;
3) if the vessel sinks or suffers some mechanical/electrical failure of equipment.

DSC Acknowledgement

The whole purpose of DSC automatic distress alerting is that well organized shore rescue services are called into action immediately. Therefore any yachtsman whose ship is fitted with DSC VHF and who receives a DSC distress alert, must *not* actively respond, even though his equipment may tell him to do so: his immediate response to such a signal

should be a listening watch on channel 16.

The automatic 'acknowledge' signal from a coast radio station will normally be received by the distressed vessel, and all others in the area, in a very short time. The ship's equipment will respond by way of a visual light and a sound signal, and maybe an automatic tuning to channel 16.

Distress Message

Whatever the distressed vessel's equipment does in response to an acknowledgement, the master must, after a short period – some 20 seconds – ensure that a voice distress message is transmitted on channel 16. The message should be in the following format:

> MAYDAY MAYDAY MAYDAY
> THIS IS... (vessel's name, three times)
> MAYDAY
> MMSI and name or callsign
> Position and nature of distress
> Assistance wanted
> Crew's description
> OVER

It is of course possible that a yacht, not itself in distress, may receive a DSC distress alert and not receive a coast radio station acknowledgement, nor hear subsequent distress traffic on channel 16; in which case, after a suitable interval, the yacht may call the vessel in distress, verbally on 16, in the following manner:

> MAYDAY
> MMSI of vessel in distress, or its name/callsign (three times)
> THIS IS...

MMSI of own vessel or
name/callsign (three times)
RECEIVED MAYDAY
OVER

Having acknowledged the DSC alert by voice, you should now transmit a DSC *urgency alert*. Then, whether a coast radio station acknowledges by DSC or not, transmit a *distress relay* call on channel 16 as follows:

MAYDAY RELAY, three times
THIS IS MMSI, once, or name three times
RECEIVED MAYDAY FROM MMSI and name of distressed vessel
BEGINS... repeat message as received

Urgency and Safety

In a similar vein to distress, the initial urgency, safety and routine traffic call is made by DSC on channel 70. The type of call is selected from a displayed menu. Following the DSC urgency call, the message itself is made on 16, and in the following form:

PAN PAN, three times
ALL STATIONS
THIS IS MMSI, callsign or name,
once
Position
Type of urgency
Assistance required
etc
OVER

Following a DSC safety call, the message itself is made on a working channel specified in the DSC call, as:

SECUITE, three times
ALL STATIONS
THIS IS MMSI, callsign or name,
once
Text of safety message

Safety messages are not normally acknowledged.

Routine Traffic

Routine is selected from the menu. The ship, group of ships, or ships in a selected area are specified by the appropriate MMSI number, and the working channel to be used is stated. The DSC call is made, followed by the routine traffic on the defined working channel. When you receive a routine call from another station, it is accepted practice now to select DSC acknowledgement and transmit it, including within it your ability or otherwise to comply with the requested working channel.

Cospas-Sart

This satellite 'search and rescue' system relies on at least four satellites in near pole-to-pole orbit, spaced at equal intervals around the globe. The earth's spin on its own axis ensures that the four satellites give world-wide coverage.

When a 406 EPIRB or beacon is purchased it must be registered before it can be of any use to its owner.

Beacon transmissions are detected and part-processed by the Cospas satellites before being down-linked to 'local user terminals' (LUTs), which complete the processing of the signals to determine the beacon's position. This last is determined by using 'Doppler shift' (the relative motion between satellite and beacon).

The data is relayed via 'mission control centres' (MCCs) to a 'rescue coordination centre' (RCC).

An important feature of the 406 EPIRB is the addition of a coded message giving the country of origin, the identification of the vessel and, optionally, position data from on-board navigation equipment. (The Cospas satellites compute the beacon's position using Doppler shift – however, this gives only an approximate position: tests have shown a location accuracy of just 87 per cent within 5km (3 miles). Connecting the beacon to an on-board GPS can improve this accuracy to a few hundred metres or less.)

An auxiliary transmitter can be included to enable suitably equipped search and rescue vessels to 'home in' on the EPIRB. The beacon is activated either manually or automatically by shock or immersion.

In a 1990 exercise the average processing time for the first alert message was forty-three minutes.

In some cases the 406 EPIRB has an additional 'homing' transponder, which saves having to acquire a separate 'search and rescue transponder' (Sart).

The 406 EPIRB or separate Sart is taken into the life-raft when abandoning ship. The Sart will respond to a search vessel's 3cm radar pulses (frequency 9GHz) by transmitting a swept frequency signal. This signal shows up on the rescue vessel's radar screen as a distinctive line of twenty dots extending out from the Sart's position towards the rescue vessel along its bearing line; the Sart should respond at a range of approximately 5 n. miles. At approximately 1 n. mile the series of dots or blips changes to concentric arcs. As the distance closes, the arcs form into complete concentric circles. One most attrac-tive extra feature of the Sart is the fitting of an audible signal and small light, both of which are activated when the Sart responds to the search vessel's radar; to persons in distress this must be very com-forting, the nightmare of being alone and frightened somewhat lessened by know-ing that they are being observed on the radar screen by a skilled and experienced rescue crew.

Fig. 45 illustrates the basic concept of the Cospas system, and the following two reports demonstrate its usefulness to the sailor in distress.

A Family Rescued in the South Atlantic

A family comprising mother, father and two children were sailing from Argentina to the Falkland Islands on board their 43ft yacht when they were hit by a storm in January this year. On the 10th of that month, at about 7am local time, a huge wave capsized the boat, smashing the mizzen mast and hurling equipment, charts and utensils around the cabin. At 8pm, with the family still cleaning up, a second freak wave knocked them over again. The main mast was now useless too, snapped off six feet above the deck. They tried unsuccessfully to start the aux-iliary engine, and could not get the radio working. Fortunately they had a 406 MHz Cospas-Sarsat EPIRB, and it had been reg-istered, which meant that search and res-cue (SAR) authorities could quickly verify with onshore contacts the approxi-mate whereabouts of a vessel.

When the EPIRB was activated, its sig-nal was received through the Cospas-Sarsat satellite system and the position

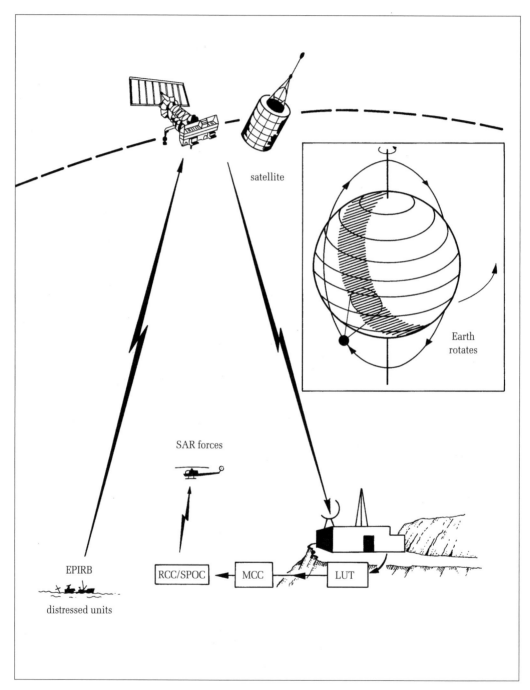

Fig 45 Basic concept of the Cospas-Sarsat System for the distressed yachtie.
Insert: One satellite; polar orbit plus earth's rotation.

was passed to the SAR forces in the Falkland Islands. However, severe weather conditions in the Falklands made it impossible initially to launch a search aircraft; this meant that later, SAR planes had to cover a large search area because of the possibility of survivors having taken to the life-rafts. As soon as it became feasible, a fixed-wing aircraft was launched to search, followed by a Sea King helicopter. An updated position for the EPIRB, received through the satellites, was passed to the aircraft.

Provided with the latest position, the aircraft found the yacht, even though it was night time; moreover it was rolling 70° from the vertical in a thirty-foot swell. Despite this, the helicopter crew lifted all four to safety. The Schinas Cospas-Sarsat 406 MHz EPIRB was their last means of transmitting a distress alert.

Immediate 406 MHz Alert

At 10:11am on 5 June 1995, the American geostationary GORS-8 satellite relayed a Cospas-Sarsat 406 MHz alert to the Spanish ground-receiving station at Maspalomas, Grand Canaria. The message contained the beacon identity belonging to a UK vessel, although no location information was available at that point. Because the beacon had been registered at the time of purchase, an enquiry to the UK beacon register database at the Cospas-Sarsat Mission Control Centre, Plymouth, quickly established, through the emergency contact given on the registration form, that the beacon was on the yacht *Severalles Challenge* bound for the Azores. Search and rescue officers in Spain and the UK estimated that the yacht could be off north-west Spain. As a

result of this information, a Spanish helicopter *Helimer Galicia* began the search.

At 11:00am, the polar-orbiting Cospas-Sarsat system computed the position of the beacon as 110 miles north-west of La Coruna, in Spain. This information was passed to the helicopter, which arrived at the location and rescued two persons from the overturned yacht.

Bad sea conditions had overturned the yacht suddenly, so the automatically activated EPIRB provided the only alert. The rescue was expedited thanks to three factors: first, the rapid detection of the alert through the geostationary satellite; second, the 406 MHz being registered, and twenty-four-hour, on-shore emergency contacts being provided; and third, the time saved in searching, due to the combined use of geostationary and polar-orbiting systems.

MF and HF Working

In addition to the above VHF DSC and EPIRB equipment, the 'blue-water' yachtsman sailing in waters outside the A1 area may also fit an MF/HF transceiver: MF (200–300kHz) has a coverage of some 300 n. miles by ground wave propagation, and HF (3–30 MHz) has world-wide transmission and reception by means of sky wave propagation. Additionally the Inmarsat satellite system is available.

Distress alerts may be sent on any of the following DSC frequencies:

MF band(kHz)	HF band(kHz)	VHF band(MHz)
2,175.5 kHz	4,207.5	156.525 (70)
	6,312	
	8,414.5	
	12,577	
	16,804.5	

When a DSC call is made it is always in the form described above, under VHF DSC. The call will include the type of subsequent communication, usually RT.

When the alerting vessel receives the acknowledgement, usually from a coast radio station, the transceiver is tuned, sometimes automatically, to the associated RT frequency in the same band as shown below:

Band	DSC distress/safety	RT distress/safety
MF	2,187.5	2,182.0
HF(4MHz)	4,207.5	4.125.0
HF(6MHz)	6,312.0	6,215.0
HF(8MHz)	8,414.5	8,291.0
HF(12MHz)	12,577.0	12,290.0
HF(16MHz)	16,804.5	16,420.0
VHF	Ch. 70	Ch. 16

For example, a DSC distress alert on the MF band is transmitted on 2,187.5 kHz; when a DSC acknowledgement is received, the distress message is transmitted on 2,182.0 kHz, its form being as described above, under Distress Message. In fact on MF, HF and VHF, the DSC alerting for distress, urgency and safety and the subsequent RT distress, urgency or safety message is always of the same form.

In general, mobile stations do not transmit DSC acknowledgements, the whole purpose – as previously stated – of a DSC alert being to activate a suitably equipped, shore-based Rescue Coordinating Centre. Yachts are not obliged to fit DSC equipment: the SOLAS convention requires only that commercial ships over 300 tons on international passages have equipment of GMDSS compliance by 1999, or they will not be allowed to sail.

When a yacht receives a DSC alert he is obliged to tune to the associated RT chan-

nel or frequency and listen out for any subsequent call and message.

It is extremely unlikely that a yacht can render any assistance at all, unless to another yacht in reasonably close proximity; in which case RT is the obvious means of communication.

Inmarsat-C

As we have seen, four ocean areas are defined and monitored by geostationary satellites, these providing the space component of this system. The 'C' version of the Inmarsat satellite service is the only one suitable for yachts, the aerial being relatively small, and more importantly, omnidirectional – that is, it does not have to be positioned and repositioned at each change of working area. The system offers DSC alerting and a digital satellite message service – *not*, repeat *not* voice. A ship's Inmarsat terminal is usually fitted with a pc to handle keyboard and display functions; a DSC alert button is part of the ship's equipment, and the subsequent distress call and message is implemented on the keyboard. There is usually a GPS interface, and since an integral part of Inmarsat-C equipment is the reception of 'maritime safety information' (MSI), it will be most useful to the long-range sailor far from land. Fig. 46 shows the basic Inmarsat system.

Accidental DSC Distress Alert

It is absolutely essential that following an accidental false DSC distress transmis-

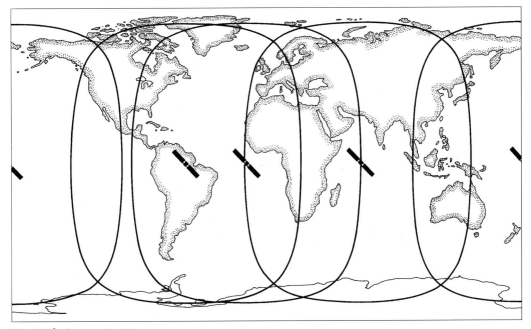

Fig. 46 The Inmarsat system.

sion you cancel the button manually and transmit an ALL STATIONS call cancelling the distress alert on the appropriate RT frequency. State in this message the vessel's MMSI, name and callsign, and state that you are cancelling the false DSC alert sent, giving the date and time of the accidental transmission.

Following the accidental activation of an Inmarsat distress or EPIRB, you must immediately notify the appropriate RCC or coast radio station.

12

WEATHER FORECASTING

The UK's weather results from the air masses which pass over it, masses which originate in permanent or semi-permanent areas of high and low pressure at various locations across the globe. The three most important characteristics of an air mass are temperature, pressure and humidity, and in any air mass both temperature and humidity fall very rapidly with increasing height. These values change much more slowly in the horizontal plane, however, and may remain the same over several hundred, if not several thousands of square miles. Over certain land or sea masses the whole air mass will have particular values of temperature, pressure and humidity in the horizontal plane, values which are unique to that area. This is because such air masses are formed in regions where the sea or the earth's temperature is reasonably constant and the winds are light, so the overlying air remains in the area long enough to take up the individual values of these three important properties. Such areas are known as 'air mass source regions'. As far as the UK is concerned, one very important source region is the permanent Azores high pressure zone; other sources are snow-covered continents,

large desert areas such as the Sahara, and the polar continents and oceans.

Air masses are classified according to their source region, the four most important ones being: 1) maritime polar (mP); 2) continental polar (cP); 3) maritime tropical (mT); 4) continental tropical (cT) (see Fig. 47).

Air Mass Properties

Air masses 1 and 2 above are obviously cold, and even colder in winter, with the continental-sourced ones the coldest of all. It is a fact that cold air is dense and cannot hold water vapour, therefore mP and cP are cold and dry air masses. By comparison air masses 3 and 4 are very warm, and may hold a lot of water in suspension, particularly those sourced over oceans; these masses are therefore said to be wet, and are of relatively low pressure.

Atmospheric Pressure

The average air pressure at sea level is ma (1013mb). Places such as the Azores and the polar regions have pressures which are permanently or semi-permanently higher, and here the high level air is con-

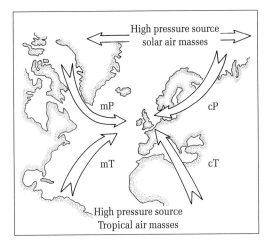

Fig. 47 Air masses arriving at UK.

tinually descending through the troposphere. The equator and areas of approximately 60° latitude have air pressures which are lower than the average, and here the surface air is continually rising through the air above it. This is because the air is heated at the equator surface, and so it increases in temperature and reduces in pressure, and is therefore caused to ascend (through the air above it). Where air is heated over the equatorial oceans it will evaporate surrounding water, thereby becoming much more humid than its continental equivalent. When these rising air masses reach the tropopause they cease rising and move polewards.

Since we are only concerned here with the northern hemisphere, we will deal only with the high level air moving towards the North Pole. Part of this air remains at high level and becomes the *jet stream* of higher latitudes; the other part of it, cooling as it moves northwards, descends very slowly to the earth's surface where it forms high pressure air masses. The Azores is one such area, and

one which has a significant effect on the climate of the UK. Once at the surface the air moves away to areas of lower pressure, some returning to the equator as the north-east tradewinds, the rest moving northwards to become the UK's south-westerlies.

When attempting to depict weather patterns cartographically, meteorologists draw lines to indicate those areas of equal atmospheric pressure surrounding areas of high and low pressure: these are known as isobars.

The Coriolis Effect

The rotation of the earth exerts a force on the air moving over its surface which turns it to the right in the northern hemisphere: this is called the Coriolis effect. One result of Coriolis is that the high level air moving northwards is deflected to such an extent that at latitudes 30° to 60° some of it becomes the high level, eastward-travelling jet stream. A second result of Coriolis is that the descending air at the Azores is deflected so much to the right as it falls that eventually it runs parallel to the isobars. However, as it falls it becomes subjected to surface friction, slows, and moves out across the isobars, at approximately 15° over the sea and some 30° over the land. (See Fig. 48.) This is explained more fully below.

As mentioned above, it is important to realize that the air-mass characteristics of

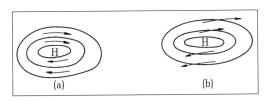

Fig. 48 Surface friction.

temperature, pressure and humidity can vary very considerably between air masses, so much so that they tend to remain as autonomous units.

Hot-Spots

Although the equatorial region is the major low pressure area of the world, other tropical and sub-tropical land and sea sectors have local, sun-heated hot-spots where the surface air is warmed by conduction, causing it to expand and rise. The centres of such a zone become low in air pressure and may therefore be surrounded by isobars of increasing pressure away from the centre. (See Fig. 49.)

Wind

In the region of the North Atlantic – latitudes 30°N and higher – many air masses of distinctly individual characteristics are present, largely as a result of the way in which these masses are formed. There are high-pressure air masses, with their internal clockwise-rotating air slowly descending to the surface; and also individual low-pressure air masses, whose internal anticlockwise-rotating, ascending air is sucked away at high level by the jet stream. To reiterate: at high altitudes air is

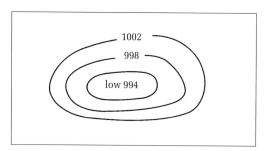

Fig. 49 Low-pressure air mass.

converging into a high-pressure air mass, spiralling clockwise downwards, and diverging at the surface; and in low-pressure air masses, the surface air converges, spirals upwards in an anticlockwise direction, then diverges at the tropopause.

In general, air tends to move directly from high to low air-pressure regions under what is called the pressure gradient; its speed is directly related to the difference in pressure, and its strength is indicated by the closeness of the isobars. However, as we have seen, air moving over our rotating earth is subjected to the Coriolis effect, whereby the air streams in the northern hemisphere are deflected to the right, the maximum deflection occurring when the air is flowing parallel to the isobars – this represents the balance point between Coriolis and pressure gradient. And as we have also seen, in associated high- and low-pressure air-mass systems, the high-level descending air moving parallel to the isobars in the high-pressure air mass, eventually becomes influenced by ground or sea-level friction. Low-altitude surface friction reduces the air speed, thus reducing the Coriolis force, and this causes the air to move out across the lower-pressure isobars and in towards the centre of the associated low-pressure air mass; from here it ascends through the upper layers of air to be sucked away by the high-level jet stream. (See Fig. 50.)

Polar-Sourced Air Masses

Air at the poles, at all heights, loses more heat by radiation than it gains indirectly from the sun. Such areas are therefore source regions of very dry, cold and dense high-pressure air masses. As the air

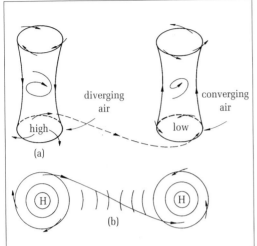

Fig. 50 Pressure gradient.

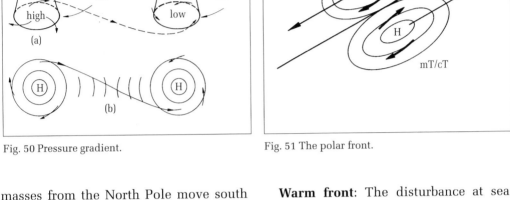

Fig. 51 The polar front.

masses from the North Pole move south they are subjected to Coriolis and are deflected to the right, becoming the UK's north-easterlies.

The Polar Front

The cold north-easterlies sourced at the poles meet the warm south-westerlies sourced at the Azores at approximately the latitude of the UK (see Fig. 51), and their line of meeting is called the 'polar front'. Due to the vastly different characteristics of these two types of air mass, their meeting can be quite dramatic, producing, as we shall see, those delightful depressions which so often dominate our weather. The two air masses will not merge, they will slide past each other, touching at their boundaries which are both physical and definite. The resulting friction may/will slow down the air in each air-mass boundary layer, setting up eddies which cause the formation of a warm and a cold front:

Warm front: The disturbance at sea level along the polar front causes the warmer, lower pressure south-westerly air mass to move up and over the much denser north-easterlies, the colder air acting like a wedge with the warmer air moving up the incline (see Fig. 52).

Cold front: As the warm front is forming, the cold, dense air of the north-easterlies moves into the warm air region and quite literally lifts the warm air up and out of the way. It is a much more brutal incursion, the surface cold front moving relatively much more quickly than the warm front (Fig. 52).

A plan view of the developing fronts is shown at Fig. 53. The whole disturbance is moving north-easterly along the polar front, and is also rotating anticlockwise about the original, now low-pressure perturbation on the front. Typically, the depression develops in the following way: the warm air continues to be moved up over the colder, but the faster-moving cold front catches up with the warm one, initially at the centre of the depression, until finally both fronts merge. The depression is said to be occluded, when all warm air is lifted from the surface and the depression is filled.

Winds associated with a depression: Study Fig. 53 again, and remembering that surface winds move in across the isobars of a low pressure system, place yourself as an observer at position 'B': the whole system, rotating anticlockwise about 'A', will be moving north-easterly towards you. First you will experience a

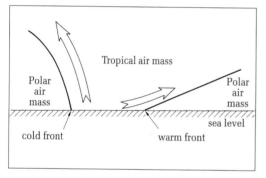

Fig. 52 Warm and cold fronts.

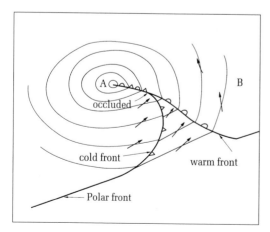

Fig. 53 Developing depression.

south-easterly wind whose strength will be related to the density of the isobars; it may back a little as the warm front approaches, but this shift may be so small as to go unnoticed. When the warm front passes, however, a very distinct shift in the wind will be noticed because it moves clockwise – that is, it 'veers', sometimes by up to 40°. The wind then remains steady as the warm sector passes over you, until as the cold front passes a second, very distinct veer may, and usually will occur.

Precipitation associated with a depression: Ahead of the warm front the warm air is rising up over the wedge-like cold air mass; this warm air may be very humid, though precisely to what extent we cannot say, since it depends on the history of any one particular mass. However, typically it will be holding some water in evaporated form, therefore as it rises it will eventually reach its dewpoint, clouds will form, and almost certainly precipitation will be present. Fig. 54 shows typical cloud formation up to 200 miles (320km) ahead of a warm front. The surface warm front itself – that is, the point of the wedge – advances into the cold air region as the warm sector air heats it. In the warm sector itself there may be rain, haze or fog, depending upon the characteristics of the particular warm air mass.

Within 50 n. miles of the approaching cold front there may very well be heavy rain – remember the abrupt way in which the undercutting, encroaching cold air mass lifts the warm sector air up and over. Heavy rain may persist for a while after the cold front passes, but thereafter the skies should clear as the dry cold air moves over the observer.

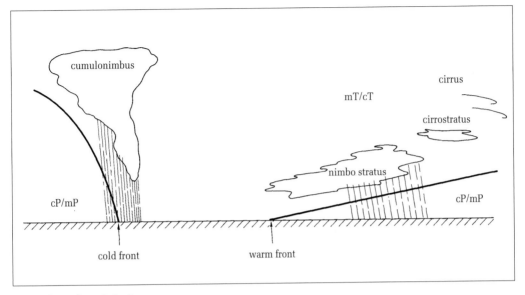

Fig. 54 Frontal precipitation.

Land and Sea Breezes

In addition to weather resulting from some combination of the four major air-mass types, weather at sea, and particularly in coastal regions, can be determined by the heating and cooling of local land masses.

During the morning of a fine sunny day, the land temperature can rise quite quickly – whereas of course the diurnal temperature of the sea changes very little. The air in immediate contact with the warming earth will heat and expand, thereby becoming less dense than the air above it: it will therefore rise. This air will be cooled as it rises, and at the tropopause will move out over the sea; continuing to cool, it will fall to the sea surface and will then move back towards the land, as a sea breeze, to fill the partial vacuum left by its original rising. The complete cycle will then be repeated, and its effects will increase throughout the

hot period of the day. In effect this sea breeze sets in at mid-morning, at about 1000–1100 local time, and it may well reach force 3–4 on the Beaufort scale by 1400, before dying away at sunset. Its effect can often be felt up to 20 n. miles offshore, and in exceptional cases 60–80 n. miles. When the shipping forecast defines the weather as 'variable 2 to 3', the yachtsman may well find that the noon sea breeze is the dominant local wind.

In the evening as the land cools, the air above it is cooled and becomes more dense, and under the influence of gravity, falls and moves out over the sea, forming a land breeze. If the land has cooled rapidly, the air forming the land breeze will be warmed by the sea, and in rising will move back over the land to form a repeating cycle in the opposite direction to the daytime sea breeze. In general the land breeze is less well developed than the sea breeze.

Fog

Fog may occur when moist, warm air is cooled. First the air becomes saturated; but if cooling increases it cannot continue to hold its moisture in suspension, and the vapour will condense into water droplets which attach themselves to the tiny solid particles – miniscule grains of sand or salt crystals – which are always present in the air. The density of the fog, or obscuration, is dictated by the density of the air-borne particles and the humidity of the air mass.

Fog is of two types: 'advection fog', formed by a maritime tropical (mT) air mass being cooled as it passes over a cold sea; and 'radiation fog', in which a warm, wet air mass lying over land is cooled by radiation as the temperature of the land below it falls rapidly during the night.

Advection Fog

An mT air mass moving towards the UK, particularly in spring or early summer when the sea temperature in the western approaches is still low, may well be cooled at its surface to such an extent that condensation occurs and fog develops. The problem with this type of fog is that in cooling, the surface air may well be colder than the air above it: that is, an 'inversion' of the normal vertical air temperature gradient is set up. It is a very stable state, such that even as daytime temperatures build up, the lower layers of air remain cold and therefore do not rise from the surface.

Advection fog is therefore persistent, and it may even require a new air mass to move into the area in which it forms in order to clear it.

Radiation Fog

Radiation fog forms over the land, particularly during those periods of clear skies and little wind. In these circumstances radiation from the land will cool the lower air, and saturation and condensation may occur, with fog forming. Gravity will move this fog downhill and out across the local sea area. Radiation fog is most likely to happen in the late and early months of the year when the land overnight can cool very quickly. Fortunately such fog will dissipate as the new day's sun heats the land, and the air in contact with it warms to the point at which it can once again evaporate the airborne water droplets.

Waking up alongside the town quay in Poole in heavy fog in September usually means that by the time a shore-side breakfast is over and the sun is up, the fog is beginning to disperse, the whole of Poole harbour appears to be visible, and the day's sailing can get under way. However, a word of caution: out over the cold sea the fog may still persist, and almost certainly there will be large banks of it just where those huge, 'yacht-seeking ferries' are lurking – so proceed with caution, and don't forget to hoist your radar reflector before you go.

Weather Forecasting

Weather forecasting is for the professional forecasters, and is not a task to be lightly undertaken by the average cruising yachtsman. The UK weather systems are generally determined by North Atlantic depressions formed far out at sea, and the above explanation of a single depression is, from a practical point of view, highly over-simplified – you need only watch television to see just how complex weather patterns can be.

Radio 4 issues weather forecasts throughout the day, and it is possible for the dedicated amateur forecaster to translate these verbal descriptions into a synoptic weather chart, complete with fronts and subsequent weather details. However, studying published weather charts from a number of daily papers, or obtaining a three- to five-day forecast from Marinecall before you sail, is by far the best option because they at least show how things may develop. Navtext is perhaps the best option of all: this is a piece of onboard equipment which, amongst other things, allows the sailor at sea to obtain weather forecast synoptic charts.

Weather Forecast Symbols

However you obtain your synoptic chart, you will need to understand the meaning of the following words and symbols:

Time: imminent, soon and later = within 6 hours, 6 to 12 hours and over 12 hours.
Visibility: good, moderate, poor, mist/haze and fog = more than 5 n. miles, 2 to 5 n. miles, 1,000m to 2 n. miles, 1,000 to 2,000m and less than 1,000m.
Air barometric pressure: steady, rising/falling slowly, rising/falling, rising/falling quickly, rising/falling v. rapidly, and now rising/falling = <0.1, 0.1 to 0.5, 1.6 to 3.5, 3.6 to 6.0, >6.0 and from rising to falling. All of these in three hours.

The Beaufort Notation:

Rain	r
Drizzle	d
Snow	s
Shower	p
Hail	h
Thunderstorm	th
Squall	q
Mist	m
Fog	f
Haze	z

13

THE INTERNATIONAL RULES FOR THE PREVENTION OF COLLISIONS AT SEA (IRPCS)

The rules are presented in five parts:

Part A: 'General', rules 1 to 3
Part B: 'Steering and Sailing', rules 4 to 19
Part C: 'Lights and Shapes', rules 20 to 31
Part D: 'Sound and Light Signals', rules 32 to 37
Part E: 'Exemptions', rule 38

There are also four annexes:

Annex I: 'The positioning and technical details of lights and shapes'
Annex II: 'Additional lights for fishing vessels fishing in close proximity'
Annex III: 'Technical details of sound signal appliances'
Annex IV: 'Distress signals'

The text in this chapter is not a comprehensive copy of the *International Rules for the Prevention of Collisions at Sea* (IRPCS). However, it should be noted that the IMO has worded the IRPCS very carefully: for example in rule 34, three short blasts on a whistle indicate that a vessel is 'operating astern propulsion', and not that she is 'going astern'. The precision of this statement in the rules is to cover situations in which very large vessels, in engaging astern propulsion, may in fact

continue to make way ahead for many nautical miles before actually stopping and going astern. The reader is strongly recommended to obtain and to study a full set of the IRPCS. The annexes to the rules are not covered here; however, please note Annex IV of the IRPCS, which describes the signals to be made by vessels in distress and in need of assistance. In this book we will merely summarize the rules, and use illustrations to show the author's understanding of them.

Part A: General

Rule 1. *Who obeys these rules?* If you are the skipper of a vessel, on the high seas or on any connected navigable waters, capable of being used for transport, then you must obey the rules except where they are modified by special rules made by the government of a state.

Rule 2. *What is the skipper's responsibility in obeying these rules?* The skipper has a responsibility to behave in all circumstances, in a good, seamanlike manner. The rules themselves are not enough, because they simply cannot cover every situation in which a collision may occur. The final decision of what avoiding action to take is up to the two skippers involved.

Rule 3. *Definitions:*
'Vessel' defines every description of watercraft; it includes non-displacement craft and seaplanes manoeuvring on the water.

'Power-driven' means any vessel, including a sailing vessel, which is being propelled by machinery.

'Sailing vessel' means any vessel being propelled by sail alone. When a vessel is motor sailing, ie her sails and the engine are both providing propulsion, she is a power vessel by these rules, and must identify herself as such.

'Vessel engaged in fishing': any vessel fishing whose fishing apparatus restricts her ability to manoeuvre. A power-driven vessel designed as a fishing vessel, going to or from the fishing ground, ie not actually fishing, is merely a power-driven vessel.

'Seaplane': any aircraft designed for manoeuvring on the water.

'Vessel not under command': any vessel which through some exceptional circumstance, ie an electrical or mechanical failure, is unable to manoeuvre according to the rules and cannot therefore keep out of your way.

'Vessel restricted in her ability to manoeuvre': any vessel which because of the nature of her work is unable to keep out of the way of other vessels. A list of such vessels is given below; however, the list is not exhaustive, and other vessels not listed here may also claim priority under this rule:

Vessels at work on navigation marks, submarine cables or pipelines, dredging, surveying, underwater operations, replenishment or transfer of people or cargo when under way, launching or recovering aircraft, mine-clearing or towing, such that the towing vessel and the tow are severely restricted in their ability to deviate from their course.

'Vessel constrained by her draught': any power-driven vessel whose draught and width severely restrict her to a particular course.

'Under way': a vessel not at anchor or made fast to the shore or aground.

'Length and breadth': a vessel's overall length and greatest breadth.

'In sight of one another': vessels which can be observed visually one from the other are said to be in sight.

'Restricted visibility': visibility reduced through fog, mist, snow, rainstorms or similar causes.

Part B: Steering and Sailing

Rule 4. This rule simply states that the following rules, 5 to 19, apply in any condition of visibility.

Rule 5. Lookout: Every vessel shall, at all times, keep a proper lookout, by sight, sound and all available means appropriate to the situation.

Rule 6. Every vessel shall proceed at a safe speed appropriate to the prevailing situation. The following factors and any other existing circumstance shall be amongst those considered in determining a safe speed:

The state of visibility, traffic density, manoeuvrability of the vessel, at night the presence of shore or other lighting including that of your own vessel, state of the wind, sea and current, proximity of navigational hazards, draught in regard to depth of water.

Vessels with operational radar in addition to the above will consider the characteristics and limitations of the radar equipment, including the radar range, the effect on the set of the sea state, weather and other sources of interference, the likelihood that small vessels and other objects including low-lying land may not be detected, the number, location and movement of other vessels detected by the radar, and the more exact assessment of visibility that may be possible when radar is used to determine the distance of vessels or objects.

Rule 7. *Risk of collision*: Every vessel shall, at all times, determine if a risk of collision exists. If there is any doubt such risk shall be deemed to exist.

Proper use of operational radar, if fitted, shall be made including long-range scanning to obtain earliest warning of risk of collision. Assumptions shall not be made based on scanty information, especially scanty radar information.

A risk of collision exists if the compass bearing of an approaching vessel does not appreciably change. A risk of collision may exist even when the compass bearing does change appreciably, particularly when approaching very large vessels, vessels towing or vessels at close range.

Rule 8. *Action to avoid collision:* Action taken to avoid a collision shall, if the circumstances permit, be positive, made in ample time and with due regard to good seamanship. Action taken to avoid a collision with another vessel should not result in another close-quarters situation. The action should result in the two vessels passing at a safe distance until they are well past and clear.

This rule emphasizes the importance of positive, early and well controlled avoiding action. Skippers of yachts in situations where another vessel has priority of passage must make it obvious to the 'stand-on' skipper that they are aware of their own 'give-way' obligation under these rules by taking avoiding action in the manner prescribed.

Rule 9. Vessels in a narrow channel or fairway shall keep as close to the outer starboard side of that channel as is safe and navigable. Vessels of less than 20m (25ft), a sailing vessel, a vessel engaged in fishing or a vessel crossing the narrow channel or fairway shall not impede the passage of a vessel which can only navigate safely within that narrow channel. The latter vessel may use at least five short and rapid blasts on a whistle if he is in doubt of the crossing vessel's intentions (see rule 34).

In a narrow channel or fairway when an overtaking vessel can only do so if the vessel to be overtaken has to take action to permit a safe passage, the overtaking vessel must indicate her intentions by issuing one of the following signals on her whistle:

Two long blasts followed by one short blast, to mean 'I intend to pass on your starboard side'.

Two long blasts followed by two short blasts, to mean 'I intend to pass on your port side' (see rule 34).

The vessel being overtaken shall, if in agreement, take such action as will allow safe passing, and will indicate her agreement by sounding one long, one short, one long, and one short blast on her whistle (see rule 34). If in doubt she will sound at least five short and rapid blasts (34) on her whistle.

This rule does not relieve the overtaking vessel of her obligations under rule 13.

A vessel nearing a bend, or anywhere that other vessels may be obscured by an obstruction, shall sound one long blast. This will be answered by any vessel approaching around the obstruction, within hearing distance, giving a long blast in return (see 34).

Vessels shall, if circumstances permit, avoid anchoring in a narrow channel.

Rule 10. *Traffic separation schemes:* A vessel joining or leaving a traffic separation scheme will normally do so at its termination, but when joining at either side shall do so at as small an angle as possible to the general flow of traffic within the scheme. When inside the scheme, a vessel, other than a vessel engaged in fishing, shall keep clear of a separation line or separation zone and shall proceed in the appropriate lane in the general direction of traffic flow for that lane.

A vessel crossing a traffic separation scheme shall do so on a heading at right angles to the general flow of traffic.

A vessel navigating near the terminations of a traffic separation scheme shall do so with extreme caution, and avoid, so far as is practical, anchoring in the area. Vessels not using the scheme shall avoid

it by as wide a margin as is possible. A vessel engaged in fishing, a vessel of less than 20m (65ft) or a sailing vessel shall not impede the safe passage of a power-driven vessel using a traffic lane.

A vessel restricted in her ability to manoeuvre when engaged in maintenance of safety of navigation or engaged in laying, servicing or taking up of a submarine cable in a traffic separation scheme is exempted from complying with this rule to the extent necessary to carry out her work.

Rule 11. This rule simply states that rules 12 to 18 are for vessels in sight of one another.

Rule 12. *Sailing vessels:* When two sailing vessels are closing with a risk of collision, one shall keep out of the way of the other as follows:

(1) When each has the wind on a different side, the vessel with the wind on her port side shall keep out of the way of the other.
(2) When each has the wind on the same side, the one to windward will keep out of the way of the other.
(3) If a vessel with the wind on her port side sees a vessel to windward and cannot determine whether the wind is on her port or starboard side, she shall keep out of the way of the other vessel.

The windward side is the one opposite to that on which the mainsail is carried, or in the case of a square-rigged vessel, the opposite side to that on which the largest fore-and-aft sail is set.

Rule 13. *Overtaking:* Any vessel coming up with another vessel from a direction more than 22.5° abaft the other vessel's beam is an overtaking vessel and shall keep out of the way of the vessel being overtaken. The overtaking vessel's obligation to keep clear does not end until she is well past and clear of the vessel being overtaken.

Rule 14. *Head-on situation:* When two power-driven vessels are meeting on reciprocal courses, or nearly so. Each shall sound a single blast and alter course to starboard, so that each passes the other on her port side.

Rule 15. *Crossing situation:* When two power-driven vessels are crossing so that a risk of collision exists, the vessel which has the other on her starboard side shall give way, and if the circumstances permit, shall avoid passing ahead of the other vessel.

Rule 16. *Action by give-way vessel:* Every give-way vessel in a 'risk of collision' situation shall take early and substantial action to keep well clear.

Rule 17. *Action of stand-on vessel:* Every stand-on vessel in a 'risk of collision' situation shall keep her course and speed. She may, however, take action to avoid collision by her action alone, as soon as it becomes clear that the give-way vessel is not taking appropriate action to keep clear. When, for any reason, the stand-on vessel finds herself so close that a collision cannot be avoided by the action of the give-way vessel, she shall take such action as will best aid to avoid collision. When taking such action she should avoid turning to port for a vessel on her own port side.

This rule needs to be fully understood. Initially when a risk of collision is recognized the stand-on skipper is obliged to maintain course and speed. However, if he observes that the give-way vessel is not complying, then he 'may' take action to avoid collision; however, should he not do so at this stage, and the situation worsens to the point that, whatever the give-way vessel now does, a collision will occur, the stand-on skipper shall take avoiding action.

This change of wording from 'obliged to stand on', through 'may take action', to 'shall take action', is one in which the good seamanship qualities of a skipper are called into action. In the final scenario a collision is almost certainly going to happen, which means lawyers, courts and someone being blamed; however, good observation and seamanship may stop it being you.

Rule 18. *Responsibilities between vessels:* Except where rules 9,10 and 13 otherwise require:

(a) A power-driven vessel under way shall keep out of the way of:
    (i) A vessel not under command.
    (ii) A vessel restricted in her ability to manoeuvre.
    (iii) A vessel engaged in fishing.
    (iv) A sailing vessel.

(b) A sailing vessel under way shall keep out of the way of:
    (i) A vessel not under command.
    (ii) A vessel restricted in her ability to manoeuvre.
    (iii) A vessel engaged in fishing.

(c) A vessel engaged in fishing when under way shall so far as possible keep out of the way of:
    (i) A vessel not under command.
    (ii) A vessel restricted in her ability to manoeuvre.

Any vessel other than one not under command or one restricted in her ability to manoeuvre shall, if the circumstances permit, avoid impeding the safe passage of a vessel constrained by her draught, exhibiting the signals of rule 28. A vessel constrained by her draught shall navigate with particular caution.

A seaplane on the water shall keep well clear of all vessels; however, where a risk of collision exists, she shall comply with the rules of this part.

Rule 19. *Conduct of vessels in restricted visibility:* This rule applies to vessels not in sight of one another, navigating in or near an area of restricted visibility.

Every vessel shall proceed at a safe speed, and a power-driven vessel shall have her engines ready for immediate manoeuvre. Any vessel which detects by radar alone that a close-quarters situation is developing with another vessel shall take avoiding action, provided that where a change of course is made she should avoid:

(i) A change of course to port for a vessel ahead of the beam except for a vessel being overtaken.
(ii) A change of course towards a vessel abeam or abaft the beam.

Except where it has been determined that a risk of collision does not exist, every vessel hearing the fog signal of another vessel ahead of her beam, or which cannot avoid a close-quarters situation with another vessel ahead of her beam, shall reduce her speed to the minimum necessary to keep her course, and if necessary will take all way off.

Part C: Lights and Shapes

Rule 20. Rules in this part shall be complied with in all weathers. Rules concerning lights shall be complied with from sunset to sunrise and during restricted visibility.

The rules concerning shapes shall be complied with during daylight.

Rule 21. *Definitions:*
(a) Masthead light: a white light over the fore-and-aft centre of the vessel showing an unbroken light from 22.5° abaft one beam through ahead to 22.5° abaft the other beam.
(b) Sidelights: a green light on the starboard side and a red light on the port side showing an unbroken light from dead ahead to 22.5° abaft the respective beam.
(c) Stern light: a white light showing an unbroken light from 22.5° abaft one beam through astern to 22.5° abaft the other beam.
(d) Towing light: a yellow light with the same characteristics as the stern light.
(e) All round light: a light showing an unbroken light over 360°.
(f) Flashing light: a light flashing at regular intervals at 120 flashes or more per minute.

Rule 22. *Visibility of lights:* Lights prescribed in these rules shall have the following minimum ranges:
(a) Vessels of 50m (164ft) or more in length:
masthead light, 6 miles (9.6km);
sidelight, 3 miles (4.8km);
stern light, 3 miles;
towing light, 3 miles;
all-round light, 3 miles.
(b) Vessels of 12m (40ft) or more, but less than 50m (164ft):

masthead light, 5 miles (8km); except where length is less than 20m (65ft), 3 miles;
sidelight, 2 miles (3.2km);
stern light, 2 miles;
towing light, 2 miles;
all-round light, 2 miles.
(c) Vessels less than 12m (40ft):
masthead light, 2 miles (3.2km);
sidelight, 1 mile (1.6km);
stern light, 2 miles;
towing light, 2 miles;
all-round light, 2 miles.
(d) In inconspicuous, partly submerged vessels or objects being towed: a white all-round light, 3 miles (4.8km).

Rule 23. Power-driven vessels under way shall exhibit the following: a masthead light forward; a second masthead light abaft of, and higher than the first, except that if less than 50m ((164ft) in length she is not obligated to carry the second masthead light but may do so; side- and stern lights.

Power-driven vessels under 12m (40ft) may carry, instead of the above, one all-round white light and sidelights; these lights may be displaced from the fore-and-aft centre line, provided that the sidelights are combined in one lantern and carried in that same displaced fore-and-aft line. Where the vessel is less than 7m (23ft) and has a maximum speed not exceeding 7 knots, she will only carry the sidelights if it is practical to do so.

Air-cushion vessels in non-displacement mode shall also carry an all-round flashing yellow light.

Rule 24. *Towing and pushing:* A power-driven vessel shall carry two masthead lights in a vertical line.

When the tow exceeds 200m (656ft) from the stern of the towing vessel to the aft end of the tow, three masthead lights in a vertical line, sidelights, stern lights, and a towing light vertically above the stern light shall be carried. Also a diamond shape where it can best be seen.

When a pushing vessel and a vessel being pushed ahead are rigidly connected in a composite unit they shall be regarded as a power vessel.

A power-driven vessel when pushing ahead or towing alongside, except as a composite unit, shall carry two masthead lights in a vertical line, sidelights and a stern light.

Power vessels towing under this rule will also carry a second masthead light abaft and higher than the vertically mounted ones as described in rule 23.

A vessel or object being towed, other than an inconspicuous, partly submerged vessel or object, shall exhibit sidelights and a stern light; and when the length of the tow exceeds 200m, a diamond shape where it can best be seen.

Provided that any number of vessels being towed alongside or pushed in a group shall be lighted as one vessel, a vessel being pushed ahead shall exhibit sidelights, and a vessel being towed alongside shall exhibit sidelights at the forward end and a stern light.

An inconspicuous, partly submerged vessel or object, or a combination of these, when being towed, shall exhibit:
If it is less than 25m (80ft) in breadth, one all-round white light at, or near, the forward and after ends, except that dracones need not exhibit the forward light.
If it is 25m or more in breadth, two additional all-round white lights at or near the extremities of its breadth.

If it exceeds 100m (328ft) in length, additional all-round white lights between those described above so that the distance between the lights shall not exceed 100m. Also a diamond shape at, or near, the aftermost part of the last vessel or object being towed, and if the length of the tow exceeds 200m (656ft), an additional diamond shape where it can best be seen as far forward as is practicable.

Where from sufficient cause it is impractical for a vessel or object being towed to exhibit the lights prescribed in this rule, all possible measures shall be taken to light the vessel or object, or at least to indicate the presence of such vessel or object.

Where from any sufficient cause it is impractical for a vessel not normally engaged in towing to display the prescribed towing lights, such vessel, when engaged in towing another vessel in distress or otherwise in need of assistance, shall take all possible measures to indicate the nature of the relationship between them as authorized in rule 36, in particular by illuminating the towing line.

Rule 25. *Sailing vessels under way and vessels under oars.*

A sailing vessel under way shall exhibit sidelights and a stern light. If the vessel is less than 20m (65ft) in length, these lights may be combined in one lantern carried at or near the top of the mast where it can best be seen. These vessels may also carry two all-round lights, a red placed vertically over a green one at or near the top of the mast, although such lights shall not be exhibited in conjunction with the combined lantern. A sailing vessel less than 7m (23ft) in length or a vessel under oars, if not carrying the lights prescribed above, shall have ready at hand an electric torch or lighted lantern showing a white light which shall be exhibited in sufficient time to prevent a collision. A vessel under sail and under engine shall exhibit forward where it can best be seen a conical shape, apex downwards.

Rule 26. *Fishing vessels:* A vessel engaged in fishing, under way or at anchor shall exhibit only the lights and shapes of this rule.

A vessel engaged in trawling: Two all-round lights in a vertical line, a green over a white. A shape consisting of two cones with their apexes together in a vertical line; a vessel of less than 20m (65ft) may instead of the cones exhibit a basket. Also a masthead light abaft and higher than the all-round green, although she is not obliged to if she is under 50m (164ft). When making way, sidelights and a stern light.

A vessel engaged in fishing other than trawling: Two all-round lights in a vertical line, a red over a white. The same shapes as a trawler. When making way, sidelights and a stern light.

When there is outlying gear extending more than 150m (492ft) horizontally from the vessel, an all-round white light or a cone apex upwards in the direction of the gear.

Vessels engaged in close proximity to other vessels engaged in fishing may exhibit additional lights as prescribed in annex II to these rules.

Rule 27. *Vessels not under command or restricted in their ability to manoeuvre.*

A vessel not under command shall exhibit two all-round red lights in a vertical line, and by day two balls in a vertical line where they can best be seen, in addition when making way sidelights and a stern light.

A vessel restricted in her ability to manoeuvre, except mine-clearing, shall exhibit three all-round lights in a vertical line, the top and bottom being red, the middle one white, and three shapes in a vertical line, the top and bottom being balls, the middle one a diamond. And when making way, masthead light or lights, sidelights and a stern light. In addition, when at anchor, the lights and shapes prescribed in rule 30.

A power-driven vessel when towing and severely restricted in her ability to deviate from her course shall in addition to her towing lights and shapes exhibit the three all-round lights and shapes prescribed in this rule.

A vessel engaged in dredging or underwater operations shall exhibit the three all-round lights and shapes of this rule, and in addition when an obstruction exists, shall exhibit two all-round red lights and two balls in a vertical line to indicate the side on which the obstruction exists, and two all-round green lights and two diamond shapes in a vertical line to indicate the side on which vessels may pass. When at anchor these same lights and shapes instead of those in rule 30.

Whenever a vessel engaged in diving operations is too small to exhibit all these lights, she shall exhibit three all-round lights in a vertical line, the highest and lowest red and the middle white, also a rigid international code flag 'A' not less than one metre in height visible all round.

A vessel engaged in mine-clearance operations, in addition to the lights of a power-driven vessel or the lights prescribed for anchoring, shall exhibit three all-round green lights or three balls, one of these at the foremast head and one at each end of the fore-yard to indicate that it is dangerous to approach within 1,000m (3,280ft).

A vessel of less than 12m (40ft), except those engaged in diving operations, shall not be required to show the lights and shapes prescribed in this rule.

Rule 28. *Vessels constrained by their draught* shall, in addition to obeying rule 23, exhibit three all-round red lights in a vertical line and a cylinder.

Rule 29. *Pilot vessels* shall exhibit at the masthead two all-round lights in a vertical line, the upper red and the lower white. And when under way, additionally stern and sidelights. And when anchored, additionally the lights of rule 30.

Rule 30. *Anchored vessels or vessels aground:* A vessel at anchor shall exhibit in the fore-part one all-round white light or a ball, and in the stern one all-round white light at a lower level. If less than 50m (164ft) she may exhibit a single all-round white light. A vessel of 100m (328ft) shall also, and others may, use her working lights to illuminate her decks.

A vessel aground shall additionally exhibit two all-round red lights in a vertical line, or three balls.

A vessel less than 7m (23ft) anchored, but not in or near a narrow channel, fairway or anchorage, or where other vessels normally navigate, shall not be required to obey this rule.

A vessel of less than 12m (40ft), when aground, shall not be required to obey this rule.

Rule 31. *Seaplane:* Where it is impractical for a seaplane to exhibit the lights and shapes described above, she shall exhibit lights and shapes as closely similar as possible.

Part D: Sound and Light Signals

Rule 32. *Definitions:* A whistle is defined in Annex III of these regulations.

A 'short blast' = a blast of about one second's duration.

A 'prolonged blast' = a blast of about four to six seconds' duration.

Rule 33. *Equipment for sound signals:* A vessel of 12m (40ft) or more shall carry a whistle and a bell, and if over 100m (328ft), in addition a gong. All of which shall comply with annex III.

A vessel less than 12m shall be provided with some means of making an efficient sound signal.

Rule 34. *Manoeuvring and warning signals.*

When vessels are in sight of one another, a power-driven vessel when under way and manoeuvring under these rules, shall indicate with her whistle:

One short blast: 'I am altering my course to starboard.'
Two short blasts: 'I am altering my course to port.'
Three short blasts: 'I am operating astern propulsion.'

These whistle signals may be supplemented by light signals using an all-round white light complying with Annex I of these regulations.

When in sight of one another in a narrow channel or fairway, a vessel intending to overtake another shall whistle:

Two prolonged blasts followed by one short to indicate: 'I intend to overtake on your starboard side'; or,
Two prolonged blasts followed by two short blasts to indicate: 'I intend to overtake on your port side.'

The vessel about to be overtaken shall indicate her agreement by the following whistle blasts:

One prolonged, one short, one prolonged and one short.

When vessels are in sight of, and approaching each other, and either vessel fails to understand the intentions or actions, or is in doubt about the sufficiency of the action of the other vessel, that vessel shall immediately issue at least five short blasts on her whistle. Such signal may be supplemented by a light signal.

A vessel nearing an area of a channel or fairway where other vessels may be obscured shall sound one prolonged blast. Such signal shall be answered by a prolonged blast by any vessel approaching around or behind the obstruction.

Rule 35. *Sound signals in restricted visibility.* In, or near, an area of restricted visibility the following signals shall be used:

A power-driven vessel making way: one prolonged blast at intervals of not more than two minutes.

When under way but stopped: two prolonged blasts with about two seconds between them at an interval of not more than 2 minutes.

A vessel not under command, a vessel restricted in her ability to manoeuvre, a vessel constrained by her draught, a sailing vessel, a vessel engaged in fishing, a vessel when engaged in fishing at anchor, a vessel restricted in her ability to manoeuvre when carrying out her work at anchor, and a vessel towing or pushing, shall, instead of the above, sound at intervals of not more than two minutes, one prolonged and two short blasts.

A vessel towed, or if more than one, the last vessel, if manned, shall sound, at not more than two-minute intervals, one prolonged and three short blasts immediately after the signal made by the tow.

A pushed and pushing vessel rigidly connected as a composite unit shall be regarded as a single power-driven vessel.

A vessel at anchor, except those mentioned above, shall ring the bell rapidly for about five seconds at intervals of not more than one minute. In a vessel of 100m (328ft) the bell shall be sounded in the fore-part of the vessel, immediately followed by the gong being sounded for about five seconds in the after part of the vessel. A vessel at anchor may additionally sound one short blast, one prolonged blast and one short blast to warn of her position. A vessel aground shall in addition give three separate and distinct strokes of the bell before and after the rapid ringing, and may also give an appropriate whistle signal.

A vessel of less than 12m (40ft) is not obliged to give the above signals, but if she does not, shall make other efficient sound signals at intervals of not more than two minutes.

A pilot vessel may in addition to the relevant signals above give an identity signal consisting of four short blasts.

Rule 36. Signals to attract attention, any vessel, to attract the attention of another vessel, may make light or sound signals that cannot be mistaken for any of the signals described in these rules, or she may direct a searchlight towards a danger. Any light used shall be such that it cannot be mistaken for a navigational aid. High intensity intermittent or revolving lights shall be avoided.

Rule 37. *Distress signals:* These signals are fully described in annex IV of these regulations.

Part E: Exemptions

Rule 38. This rule defines vessels which, complying with the rules of 1960, may be exempted from compliance with these rules.

The reader will by now realize the importance of the IRPCS. I must emphasize once again the obligation placed on a skipper to understand the full wording and content of the rules. It is also important to appreciate that the wording of these regulations may change over time. All vessels should carry an up-to-date version of the official rules, and the skipper must be aware of, and familiar with the official wording.

INDEX